Emotional Intelligence

Emotional Intelligence: The Definitive Guide, Empath: How to Thrive in Life as a Highly Sensitive, Persuasion: The Definitive Guide to Understanding Influence, Manipulation: Understanding Manipulation

By

Ryan James

Table of Contents

Book #1 - Emotional Intelligence: The Definitive Guide to Understanding Your Emotions, How to Improve Your EQ and Your Relationships

Book #2 - Empath: How to Thrive in Life as a Highly Sensitive - The Ultimate Guide to Understanding and Embracing Your Gift

Book #3 - Persuasion: The Definitive Guide to Understanding Influence, Mindcontrol and NLP

Book #4 - Manipulation: The Definitive Guide to Understanding Manipulation, MindControl and NLP

Book #1

Emotional Intelligence

The Definitive Guide to Understanding Your Emotions, How to Improve Your EQ and Your Relationships

Chapter 1:

Introduction to Emotional Intelligence

There's no escaping the concept of emotional intelligence in today's age. It has suddenly gained a massive momentum everywhere from large corporations to relationship counseling to schools and government agencies. Emotional intelligence is the new psychological health buzzword, and with good reason. It defines your emotional health and interpersonal skills, which are so vital for everyday existence.

The popular phrase was first coined by researchers Peter Salavoy and John Mayer. However, it became popular only in 1996 when researcher-psychologist Dan Goleman published a book titled, *Emotional Intelligence.* So what exactly is the concept of emotional intelligence and why is it such a clinching factor when it comes to choosing people for crucial roles and leading fulfilling personal relationships? Why is everyone feverishly looking for people with a high emotional quotient?

Emotional intelligence as described by Yale psychologist Peter Salovey and John Mayer from the University of New Hampshire is an understanding of one's emotions, empathy for other's feelings and "regulation of emotion in a manner that enhances living." This concept was shortened to make the theory more chewable and interesting for lay people by Harvard psychologist and New York Times writer Daniel Goleman. His book *Emotional Intelligence* complied years of behavioral research on processing feelings. He broadened the definition of smartness, and sought to establish that brainpower, which is measured by standardized IQ tests may not matter as much as mental qualities when it came to predicting a person's overall life success.

Goleman focused on the practical applications and how organizations can use this information to hire the right candidates, how couples could increase their chances of enjoying lasting relationships, how parents could help raise better children and how educational institutions could teach children more effectively.

Emotional Intelligence is the power to be aware of and recognize your emotions. It is the ability to correctly decipher your emotions and the impact they have on others around you. It is also about how you perceive the emotions of those around you and a high understanding about their feelings, which allows you to be a part of more fulfilling relationships.

In his path breaking book, Daniel Goleman focused on five predominant elements within the emotional intelligence framework, including self awareness, self regulation, motivation, empathy and social skills. Thus, emotional intelligence is an evolved understanding/awareness of not just your emotions but also those of others around you to manage relationships more effectively. No surprise then that emotional intelligence has overtaken other attributes such as skills, knowledge, and intelligence quotient when it comes to job recruitments. Everyone wants people with greater understanding, empathy and social skills to forge stronger relationships.

According to Daniel Goleman's blog, the concept of EQ or Emotional Quotient as a phrase is recognized in diverse languages including, German, Korean, Portuguese and Chinese. There's also a mention of religious scholars from diverse faiths communicating with the author to reinforce how the concept of emotional intelligence or emotional quotient echoes their faith's teachings. Hence, emotional intelligence can be all encompassing. It can be applied to various spheres of your life to gain more physical, mental and spiritual nourishment.

While conventional IQ attempts to evaluate a person's capacity to learn information, EQ is about a person's ability to deal with others effectively. Emotional quotient focused on evaluating soft skills such as managing relationships, showing empathy, self-awareness and social awareness. The human brain is understandably complex and it is impossible to asses a person's success quotient based on a single type of intelligence. Therefore, while IQ evaluates your technical prowess within the field of work, EQ helps you with greater emotional awareness of yourself and others.

There is absolutely no correlation between your IQ and EQ score. Some people possess an excellent academic aptitude yet struggle with handling their and other people's emotions. Haven't we all seen folks who are incredibly brainy, yet are clueless when it comes to dealing with people. IQ and EQ evaluate different types of human intelligence. While the former attempts to measure your cognitive prowess, the latter measures your emotional awareness.

Have you been so overtaken by your emotions that you regretted something you said or did later? Few people can deny this. The fact of the matter is, all of us need emotional intelligence in our everyday lives. We can all benefit from learning to manage our emotions more productively. Emotional quotient helps you forge deeper connections with friends and work associates. It leads to higher interpersonal relationship satisfaction, work performance and the ability to control stressful situations.

A heightened emotional quotient gives you the ability to identify and regulate not just your emotions but also those of others. You have no trouble empathizing with people and being aware of their responses. Emotional quotient awards you the power to manage relationships more productively, even in stressful and conflict laden situations.

Let us take an example to illustrate the concept of emotional intelligence. Ron and Bob both had a big fight with their supervisor at work. Ron didn't possess high emotional intelligence, while Bob was emotionally intelligent. On getting home, Ron began cursing and yelling at his kids who were playing noisily in the house. He acted without thinking about the impact his behavior would have on the kids.

On the other hand, when Bob returned home, he noticed his children playing nosily but told himself that they were simply being kids and doing what they do every day. They were not responsible for his problems with his supervisor or how he was feeling at the moment. Why should they be at the receiving end of his feelings when they have nothing to do with it? This is how Bob rationalizes and maintains his calm.

Did you spot the differences in approach in both these instances? Emotionally intelligent people identify their emotions, give it a good thought before reacting and behave in a more emotionally matured manner. They tend to process their emotions mentally before reacting in haste, and regretting it later, which is a typical sign of low emotional intelligence. People with low emotional intelligence react first and think about their reactions later, while people with higher emotional intelligence think before reacting.

Let us see how emotional intelligence can be practiced in some scenarios we are often confronted with. For instance, your best friend asks you for your opinion about his/her new romantic partner whom you thoroughly disapprove. He/she is extremely excited about his/her newest date, who they claim is the best thing to have ever happened to them. While they believe it's a match made in heaven, you believe it's the ultimate highway to hell. You'd obviously like to help your best friend, but you'd also like to communicate in a manner that doesn't sour things between the two of you. How do you handle the situation?

People with a high emotional quotient will start by objectively evaluating why they dislike their best friend's romantic interest. Are you plain jealous? Does their romantic relationship pose a threat to your relationship with your friend? Does their date remind you of someone whom you have had a terrible experience with? Are you brining your own experiences while evaluating their relationship?

If it is none of this and you are truly convinced that the person is just not good for your friend, you will pose more neutral questions to your friend, which will allow him/her to reflect on the answers on their own rather than go through the agony of hearing their best friend rip apart their romantic interest. If you are emotionally intelligent, you will have a few questions ready to help your friend gather the answers on their own to conclude that the journey with this person may not be as smooth as they are imagining. The idea is to help them realize things on their own without judging, criticizing and making hateful accusations. Also, as someone possessing high emotional intelligence, you must be prepared for being proved wrong.

Let us take another scenario. You have a colleague who you otherwise share a great equation with. She/he is warm, affable and pitches in whenever you require help. However, the problem here is their plainly annoying and overpowering signature perfume. The colleague's sensory receptors seem to be absent and he/she absolutely overdoes the perfume, so much that the suffocating smell makes you sick. You want to voice your objections, yet are wary of offending them because they are genuinely nice. What do you do to make the situation less awkward?

If you are an emotionally intelligent person, you will refrain from offending the other person by being too forthright and assign the blame to your allergies in a more non-confronting and less hurtful manner. Rather than blaming him/her for their tacky fragrance choices that want to make you throw up, you diplomatically assign the onus of blame on your allergies and sensitivities. "I really wish I didn't have such a fine tuned sensory perception." See what we did there? Instead of accusing the other person, you communicated your own allergy or the fact that you and not they are to be blamed for the overpowering smell.

In his bestselling book, "Emotional Intelligence – Why It Can Matter More Than IQ", researcher psychologist Daniel Goleman mentions five crucial elements that define the concept of emotional intelligence.

Self Awareness – People with high emotional intelligence are generally more self aware. They possess a solid understanding of their emotions, the impact of others behavior on their emotions and how their own behavior can affect others. They understand their emotions well enough to not let it rule them. This self awareness makes them more confident, self assured and in control. They rely on their intuition and don't allow emotions to get the better of them.

Self aware people are able to objectively analyze themselves. They are well aware of their strengths and weakness, and use them effectively to achieve the desired results in their personal and professional life. They know what aspects of themselves they need to work on. They seldom live in denial mode. Self awareness is one of the most important aspects of emotional intelligence.

There are several ways to practice self awareness such as meditation, journaling and reflection. For instance, take common stressful scenarios you cope with at work each day such as a team member failing to complete a project on time or being inundated with mails or preparing for an important last minute presentation. What are the emotions these situations elicit in you? Write down your feelings when you are in a more objective mind frame. Include personal stress inducing scenarios too such as being betrayed by a loved one or a breakdown in communication patterns. When you write objectively, it gives you a good insight of your deepest emotions.

Self Regulation – Self regulation is a person's ability to manage or control his/her emotions. Self regulators of feelings and emotions do not allow their emotions to sway them into hasty actions or words. They are seldom angry, impulsive or jealous. Their decisions are well thought out. These are the folks that actually think before acting. People with high emotional self regulation are thoughtful, secure, honest and self-assured. They act with integrity and have little trouble saying no to people where required.

Motivation – People with a high emotional quotient are always raring to go. They are firmly fixated on their goals and motivated to fulfill them. They seldom seek immediate gratification and are willing to give up short term pleasures for long term rewards. Emotionally intelligent people are more solution oriented, productive, challenge embracing and generally efficient in things they take on. Since they operate with a more positive and possibilities mind frame, they are able to stay motivated and chase their goals to fruition.

Empathy – Empathy is the crux of emotional intelligence. It is the ability to recognize and feel the emotions of others from their viewpoint. People with a high empathy quotient are brilliant at indentifying others feelings and emotions, even when they aren't very conspicuous. People with high empathy excel at relationship management, listening, and relating to the troubles of others. This makes them wonderful negotiators and leaders. They rarely judge people quickly and their lives are open books.

Social Skills – People with high social skills are effortless to deal with, which is another vital sign of emotional intelligence. They possess powerful social skills and are generally team players. Instead of obsessing over their own success, they believe in helping everyone around them shine and grow. They are very competent when it comes to managing disputes, communicating with people and building lasting relationships. Unlike folks with low emotional intelligence they do not believe in pulling down others to grow or rise in life.

Emotionally intelligent people focus on creating a win-win situation for everyone involved. They are master motivators and communicators. With their knack for handling people, these guys are the most sought after conflict resolvers and negotiators. Little wonder then than emotional intelligence is one of the most preferred attribute at the senior management level.

Social is skills is tantamount for success in every sphere of personal and professional life. In today's well-connected world, people have quick access to technical information. This is exactly why people's skills is even more crucial than technical skills. There is a greater need to be able to negotiate, identify and empathize with people in a worldwide economy. Businesses need people who can wield influence and use effective persuasion techniques by recognizing other's emotions. There is a need to communicate more clearly, and inspiring groups of people.

Organizations need competent change catalysts that can initiate or manage change efficiently. A social skill also involves conflict management, including negotiation skills and resolving differences. Collaboration, teamwork, cooperation and achieving shared goals become simpler when people possess a high emotional quotient. Pursuing collective objectives and building group synergy is effortless for people with well developed social skills and emotional intelligence.

Emotional Intelligence is a greater awareness of your own feelings, emotions and actions, and how they affect people around you. It is also about valuing others, listening to their needs and being able to empathize/identify with these folks on multiple levels. It is about feeling things from their perspective and reacting in a more appropriate and positive manner.

We all know that one person (or more than one person) in our work or personal life, who is an exceptionally good listener. Irrespective of the situation, they always say the right thing. It's almost like they instinctively know what to say. These people know how to say things to make them less offensive for people. They are caring, empathetic and considerate. Emotional intelligent folks may not necessarily have a solution to all your problems but they possess the ability to leave you feeling more positive and hopeful about the grimmest situation.

By now you've probably figured out that emotional quotient can be one of keys to success, especially in your career and interpersonal relationships. The ability to deal with people's emotions and building relationships is the essence of being a leader. Sharpening your emotional quotient can be a great way to bring out your leadership skills. The best part of emotional intelligence is that it can be developed. Even if you don't possess a very high emotional quotient, there's no reason for you to not work on it consciously and sharpen it.

While some people have an inherent gift of harnessing their emotions and weaving them seamlessly into areas such as problem solving, others keenly work on their EQ to forge more rewarding interpersonal and work relationships. They consciously develop a knack of managing and regulating their own emotions, while sharpening their ability to react to other people's emotions.

Little Cynthia watches her mommy finish a call. "Mommy, what makes you cry?" she inquires. "I am alright Cynthia, I will be ok." Cynthia runs to her room and comes back seconds later. "When I feel sad, I hold Candy in my arms", she said, handing her mother her favorite teddy bear. Cynthia knows her mother's sadness but doesn't believe in crippling her even further.

This is how emotional intelligence works. You understand a person's emotions and you don't make it more devastating for them. There is an attempt to comfort them by sharing the best you can. You don't have to judge, sermonize or lecture people. All they need is to feel secure, safe and comforted.

These guys are pros at managing their feelings. They aren't easily offended or angered even in the most stress inducing circumstances. They look at challenging situations more calmly and are more solution oriented. Emotionally intelligent folks are highly tuned in to their intuition for making important decisions. They have the ability to evaluate themselves more objectively by handling criticism rather well and knowing their areas of improvement.

When we develop the gift of better managing people's emotions and empathizing with their unique perspective, conflict resolution becomes easier. You become a better leader, negotiator, mentor, friend and other roles by being aware of the most compelling needs and desires of others. When you know the fundamental emotions that drive, it is easy to manage to manage your behavior to create a win-win situation. It becomes simpler to give people exactly what they are looking for if you are able to intuitively perceive their needs.

Jason was a highly accomplished and successful manager well-known for his knack of handling challenging organization issues and getting impressive results. He assessed situations accurately, made solid decisions, and took ownership of company projects. Jason swiftly rose from the role of a divisional manager to a senior management position within the firm.

He continued to lobby for senior organizational leadership positions and proactively sought an increase in his functional responsibilities by taking on more challenging problems. He rose to the senior management rank quickly.

Jason was confident, and others believed he would inevitably reach the echelons of management success. He did not end up in the senior executive suite. In fact, his career went downhill and the management had to look for substitutes to reassign his responsibilities. What do you think went wrong with this rather promising manager? Why did his journey to the top go off the course?

This is the story of most senior managers. While they are able to manage people at the junior management level, micromanaging managers and delegating independent authority at the senior level becomes tough. Jason was capable of getting through his behavior at the lower management level. However, once the organization became too large for his control, it was impossible to manage an efficient working relationship with senior managers.

Jason's inability to delegate authority and obsession for micromanagement were indicators of a much larger issue – he simply lacked emotional intelligence. This illustration explains why senior managers need huge reserves of emotional intelligence. Jason struggled with understanding and managing his emotions. This self awareness deficit translated into being unable to comprehend and manage other's emotions.

Jason's greatest handicap was his insecurity and fear. He feared about losing control over his organizational domain if he ceased to micromanage each aspect. His fear of being replaced if his team did their jobs only too well or being unable to control his managers if he gave them complete authority led to his dwindling fortunes. Jason became a victim of his own inability to manage his and the team's emotions.

When negative emotions are unmanageable, organizations are prone to produce disastrous results. It can result in stunted productivity, strained relationships, unmet business objectives and higher absenteeism.

According to a study, surgeons involved in malpractice suits had lesser chances of being sued if they spent an extra 3 minutes doing the following – making orienting statements, using reassuring words and communicating empathy.

Let's do a short self evaluation here to gauge your Emotional Quotient.

1. Are you able to identify your own emotions?

2. Do you quickly register the emotions of other people or are able to understand how they are feeling?

3. Can you point out exactly what triggers emotions within you?

4. Can you control or organize your emotional informational?

5. Are you willing to admit to and learn from mistakes easily?

6. Are you able to control your emotions?

7. Can you listen more than you talk or at least as equivalent to how much you talk?

8. Can you handle criticism positively?

9. Are you calm and composed under the most intense pressure situations?

These questions will help you reflect where you stand in the emotional quotient meter. However, fret not if you do not consider yourself an emotional intelligence superstar. There are tons of ways to boost your EQ.

Chapter 2:

Difference between Intelligence Quotient and Emotional Quotient

How does emotional quotient differ from intelligence quotient? The simple answer is-they measure different forms of intelligence. Your technical acumen or technical skills is a direct result of a high intelligence quotient. You've mastered your skills well, which is a reflection of well-developed cognitive abilities. However, is intelligent quotient enough to determine your success when it comes to dealing with people (unless you are cooped up on a remote island all yourself, you have to deal with people)?

While intelligence quotient measures your technical expertise, emotional quotient evaluates your ability to manage your and other people's emotions in your work and personal life. You know where every employee stands when it comes to technical prowess but do you really understand their thoughts, actions and feelings to be able to better manage your and their behavior in sync with these emotions. When we gain insights into the underlying emotional patterns of people, it becomes easier to relate to them and channelize more productive behavior. This is a fundamental difference between intelligence quotient and emotional quotient.

Ever wondered why some of the cleverest people hit a blank in their professional lives and just can't seem to climb the corporate ladder, while the less knowledgeable and inexperienced folks smoothly sail their way to professional success? We all know of people who don't exactly possess the slickest technical skills yet surprisingly manage to reach top management positions. What is it that sets them apart from their more technically competent peers? Emotional intelligence is the key. It is their ability to recognize and control their and other's emotions to build more productive relationships that helps them score.

A person's intelligence quotient demonstrates their core technical competencies, cognitive development and unusual abilities, their emotional intelligence determines their ability to identify emotions and deal with others. Your emotional quotient determines how you will deal with stress, difficult people, bullying, high pressure work situations, conflict within the team, and differences in relationships.

Intelligence is an indicator of your cognitive prowess such as logical thinking, analytical reasoning, memorizing information, solving problems, verbal abilities, creative thinking and much more. Emotional intelligence is controlling your and other's emotions for creating optimally positive circumstances. Starkly different from your ability to comprehend words and numbers, emotional quotient helps you develop healthy interpersonal relationships in your personal and work life.

Emotional intelligence can include stress management, intuition, emotional flexibility, empathy, honestly and more. Emotional quotient highlights your and others emotions with respect to changing circumstances and people, while intelligence quotient is all about cognitive abilities.

While intelligence quotient can determine your success during your academic stint, emotional quotient is vital for all round success in life. You may excel as a student if you possess a high intelligence quotient. However to attain overall success in life, you need a high emotional quotient.

Research has indicated that there are five fundamental skills that distinguish the star performers from low performers. These skills are empathy, self-awareness, assertiveness, problem solving and happiness. Potential recruits who score high on these five attributes are 2.7 times likelier to succeed than folks who bag low scores.

So, why is emotional quotient so closely associated with a person's chances of becoming successful in life? The answer is – awareness of emotions and ability to express themselves confidently. Emotionally intelligent people are experts in gauging people's emotions and altering their pitches/presentations accordingly. Little wonder then that emotionally intelligence is so vital for people in sales, customer service, counseling and other industries.

For instance, a study closely followed the recruitment of sales personnel for cosmetic giant L'Oreal based on their emotional skills. It was observed that these emotionally competent sales people outdid other salespersons by a whopping $91,370 to amass a net revenue growth of $ 2,558, 360. In another research, a national insurance firm discovered that salespersons who were low on emotional skills like initiative, confidence and empathy sold far less policies (average premium of $54,000) that agents who scored high on emotional skills (average premium of $114,000). You get the picture, right? When you show high emotional competencies by being proactive, self confident and empathetic, you are able to connect to potential buyers and help them buy rather than simply sell.

In the workplace, intelligence quotient helps for analyzing, connecting the dots and undertaking research and development. Emotional intelligence is about forging a strong team spirit, leadership, building successful professional relationships, collaboration, service and initiative. Emotional quotient can be gained and enhanced as opposed to intelligence quotient, which is a more inborn and hereditary characteristic.

The goal for businesses isn't to simply hire people who are intellectually competent, but lack emotional or people skills. Today's competitive and social interactions dominated world demands workers who are smart (that's a given), and endowed with more thoughtfulness. The ideal candidate is a combination of emotional intelligence and general intelligence. Since all candidates applying for a position possess more or less the same technical competence, emotional intelligence often becomes a clinching factor when it comes to selecting people for important roles.

Standford-Binet, Woodcock-Johnson Tests of Cognitive abilities and Wechsler are some popular intelligence quotient tests, while Mayer-Salovey-Caruso Test and Daniel Goleman model score test are popular emotional intelligence assessment tests. An Intelligence Quotient test generally involves a collection of standardized questions where participants are assigned precise scores based on their answers. These scores are evaluated with respect to average scores within the age group to establish a person's intellectual capabilities.

Emotional quotient tests, on the other hand, are more challenging to administer because feelings and emotional skills are tougher to depict numerically. While intelligence quotient questions have a definite answer for every question, emotional quotient tests tend to be more subjective and require greater evaluation effort. Unlike IQ tests, there aren't any right or wrong answers. Respondents may not answer questions honestly simply to rank high or may adjust their responses according to what they are currently experiencing, which makes these results more skewed. There may be a tendency on part of the participant to say exactly what the evaluators want to hear rather than responding truthfully.

People possessing a high intelligence quotient are excellent at conducting tasks. They are quick absorbers of new skills and information. However, if they have a low emotional quotient, they tend to overlook their and other's feelings. For instance, when something doesn't turn out according to the way they wanted, these folks tend to lose their temper and lash out at people. While someone who is high on emotional intelligence will learn to control their emotions and get along with people around them. They are extremely effective when it comes to working as a team or working in a leadership role.

The concept of emotional intelligence has gained such a strong momentum that it has impacted a large a large number of areas including the corporate world. Several top organizations have now made emotional intelligence tests mandatory as part of the hiring process, along with intelligence quotient.

In personal relationships, 90 percent of the issues arise due to lack of emotional intelligence. Everything revolves around empathy, self awareness, awareness of the other person's emotions, understanding, communication patterns and the likes, which are all components of emotional intelligence.

Emotional quotient is not the antithesis of intelligence quotient. They aren't mutually exclusive. Some folks possess both in huge quantities, while others possess neither. Psychologists are keener to explore how the two attributes balance each other. For instance, how your ability to deal with stress impacts your ability to focus or learn new information.

Chapter 3:

Benefits of Emotional Intelligence

As discussed earlier, emotional intelligence is our ability to manage our and other's emotions by discriminating among these feelings, and using the information to guide our words, thoughts and actions. To cut a long story short, emotional intelligence is an aggregation of your mental and emotional skills. Emotionally intelligent people enjoy a multitude of benefits in all spheres of life including relationships, career and social life. Here are some ways in which your life can be impacted or benefited if you consciously focus on developing high emotional intelligence.

Stellar Productivity

Emotional intelligence has a high correlation with an individual's work performance. Research has revealed that emotional intelligence is twice as crucial as technical/cognitive abilities even among professions such as engineering. Emotionally intelligent managers, supervisors and leaders are way more effective in managing teams, motivating people and negotiating.

They create a more positive atmosphere with happier workers, who are an asset to any organization. Happier workers translate into higher morale, low absenteeism, reduced attrition rate and higher productivity. This leads to happier customers, more sales and higher profits. Thus emotional intelligence is an invaluable trait when it comes to success at the workplace. Whilst everyone within an organization possesses more or less the same technical competency and educational qualifications, only a few rise up the corporate ladder because of their ability to manage people and their emotions.

An emotionally intelligent leader who understands the true value of identifying and managing emotions can empower his/her subordinates with these skills on a daily basis. Discipline or self regulation is essential when it comes to keeping your emotions in check, avoiding panic, remaining calm and being an asset to the team. Emotionally intelligent folks have little trouble in recognizing and managing potentially destructive emotions that can create stress and lower productivity. The approach is calmer, more confident and efficient. Rather than experiencing a more touchy view, these folks depend on their ability to possess a more realistic view of themselves and others.

Coping With Life Challenges

Don't you sometimes look at some people and wonder how they are able to stay afloat through the most challenging situations and emerge even more successful than before? Chances are, these guys score high on emotional intelligence. Emotionally intelligent folks have the ability to calm their body and mind to view things from a clearer and more objective perspective. Their acts are more mindful and less panic struck.

Greater calmness, objectivity and clarity award you more resilience where life's challenges are concerned. Think about the kungfu fighter who can take on the most powerful opponents by constantly working on martial arts skills. Emotional intelligence equips you with those skills to take on the toughest challenges life throws at you with resilience.

Greater Compassion in Personal and Work Life

One of the best benefits of high emotional intelligence is your ability to demonstrate more compassion for others both in the personal and professional sphere. This compassion allows them to connect with people at much deeper levels to forge meaningful relationships. Compassion can be manifested in several ways, including helping someone dealing with a personal issue by taking on their responsibilities or making small everyday decisions for the comfort/convenience of your employees.

Compassion helps you meaningfully connect with people both in your personal and professional life. You are able to reach out to people efficiently, forge more mutually fulfilling relationships and create an atmosphere of harmony and productivity. Emotional intelligence awards you greater compassion in dealing with people in various personal professional and social scenarios.

Boosted Leadership Skills

Emotionally intelligent folks possess a highly evolved ability in recognizing and understanding factors that drive others, which makes them amazing leaders. They are able to make the most of this invaluable information to strengthen their loyalty and forge stronger relationships with people. A competent leader is intuitively tuned in to the most compelling aspirations and desires of his followers. He knows the "hot buttons" of his employees and exactly how to channelize these "hot buttons" to increase overall productivity and positivity within the work environment.

Emotionally intelligent leaders know how to channelize this information for extracting better performance/productivity from people and keeping them happy. People with a high emotional quotient excel at recognizing the strengths and weaknesses of people and harnessing an individual's virtues for benefiting the team.

High emotional intelligence creates better leaders who are able to inspire greater faith and loyalty by using their team's or follower's or emotional range. They are more aware of their emotions, which allow emotionally intelligent folks to create a harmonious environment. Practicing emotional intelligence makes you a better leader.

Did you know that 67% of all competencies said to be fundamental for high performance in the professional sphere is emotional intelligence? Take the example of the world's most successful CEOs. Amazon's Jeff Bezos passionately talks about getting right into the hearts of his customers in a 2009 YouTube video while announcing the company's Zappos acquisition. When Howard Schultz of Starbucks was a child, his father lost a health insurance claim. This turned him into one of the most empathetic CEOs, who is well known showing his employees thoughtfulness by offering generous healthcare rewards. Little wonder then that these folks are as successful as they are. They understand the emotional pulse of their employees and customers to keep them emotionally gratified.

Emotional intelligence helps in building emotional maturity, boosting social intelligence, preventing relationship problems, enhancing interpersonal communication, helping control emotions, dealing with stress, influencing leadership, helping authorities make sound business change decisions, supporting staff and controlling resistance to change.

Lower Chances of Addiction and Other Emotional Disorders

Addictions are generally a direct result of our inability to cope with emotions. People who struggle to come to terms with their emotions use addiction as a mechanism to avoid the more underlying and deeper prevailing issues. When you fail to recognize and manage negative emotions, there develops an unfortunate pattern of dependency on external factors such as food, nicotine, substance, alcohol, porn and the likes. Addiction is just a means to escape from emotions you aren't willing to deal with.

Emotionally intelligent folks are lesser prone to addiction because of their awareness of their emotions and the ability to manage these emotions. They have a solid understanding of their feelings, and do not struggle to deal with it. Since emotional intelligence makes you happier, more confident and balanced, there is a lesser propensity for dependence on destructive coping mechanisms. They adapt more easily to challenges and changing scenarios in life. Emotionally intelligent people are competent in resolving differences and coming up with more positive solutions. Since they display such a high understanding of their and other's emotions, it becomes easier for them to deal with conflicts.

Emotionally healthy people are less prone to be victims of drug abuse or binge eating disorders, which predominantly originate from much deeper psychological issues.

Boosted Employee Morale and Lower Attrition

Morale may be an intangible concept in the corporate world but its effects are highly measureable. You may not realize the value of a high morale when it's there, but you will definitely know when it's missing. Think about the lateness, early departures, attrition, sick leaves your company suffers from. When leaders take the time to build emotional intelligence and connect with their team members, it reflects in the employee morale.

Emotionally intelligent leaders who build stronger emotional ties with subordinates witness improvement in the team's morale, lower measureable absenteeism, a higher team spirit and a greater desire to contribute to an organization's success. The emotional intelligence skill building cost can be minimal. However, the return on investment can be extremely high.

Let's get real here and call a spade a spade. Employees do not really quit roles, they quit senior managers. It is about escaping people and not positions. Emotionally intelligent leaders, who recognize emotional triggers, quickly pick up emotional clues of their team members and "customize" their approach to each member's unique emotional make-up and motivation will experience greater success in retaining employees. This should not be mistaken with not doing justice to one's own voice or feelings. It simply means, presenting an accurate emotional response towards each team member to treat them with greater compassion, respect and empathy.

The problem with most managers who do not understand the concept of emotional intelligence is that they use a one size fits all approach for dealing with all employees, without understanding the emotional framework, motivators and goals of individual team members. This one size fits all approach does not produce flattering results because personalities vary. Some people are more intrinsically motivated, while others thrive on extrinsic motivation. Some folks are quick to reveal their emotions; others aren't very comfortable sharing their feelings. Once you understand the emotional make-up of people, it becomes easy to deal with them more efficiently.

Fine Communication Skills

People with a well developed emotional quotient are more efficient when it comes to expressing themselves. They possess the ability to listen attentively to other people's verbal clues, while also tuning in to their non verbal communication. They know exactly what to say to channelize people's strengths. They use the right words and non verbal signals to help people feel at ease. There is little scope for misunderstanding whilst communicating with a person who has high emotional intelligence.

 Emotionally intelligent people are well aware about the most compelling emotional triggers of the people around them. They know exactly how to inspire people to act. People who are able to communicate by emotionally connecting with are far more effective than technically competent folks who fail to demonstrate empathy while communicating with people. Emotional intelligence awards you better response skills.

Chapter 4:

Proven Tips to Boost Your Emotional Intelligence

After gaining a thorough understanding of emotional intelligence and its benefits, the million dollar question is – is it really possible to improve one's emotional intelligence or emotional quotient? Is it possible from struggling to cope with your and other's emotions to being a rockstar at understanding emotions?

With all its advantages, who wouldn't want high emotional intelligence? Who wouldn't want greater professional success, business potential, leadership skills, relationship gratification, humor, good healthy, positivity and happiness around them? Think about an antidote that beats stress, helps you form rewarding relationships with people and much more.

Take any coaching intervention program, and it will generally highlight some aspect of emotional intelligence in the name of interpersonal skills or social/soft skills. The most compelling reason for this is that, while intelligence quotient is tough to change, emotional quotient can be acquired with training and consistent practice. So, the good news is that even if you do not consider yourself very emotionally evolved, there is plenty of scope to boost your emotional quotient with practice, training and conscious effort.

The best part about enhancing your emotional intelligence is that it can be practiced in your everyday life. For instance, if you are short tempered, start by showing greater empathy or being a more considerate listener.

Emotional Quotient Is Not Rigid

Though our capacity to recognize and handle our and other's emotions is largely determined by childhood experiences, heredity and other factors, it isn't rigid. We can alter our ability to comprehend and manage emotions over the long term with the right coaching and dedication. You can change of course, however, the question is do you want to change? Are you willing to put in the effort required to be more emotionally intelligent? Sometimes, while you may successfully be able to manage your external emotions, you may still grapple with emotions you do not manage to display on the outside.

While some folks are naturally positive, calm and social, others can be plain grumpy, egoistic, shy or insecure. However, no trait is unchangeable. If you truly want to change an aspect of your personality, you can. Emotional intelligence naturally increases with age, without any intervention. This is the rationale behind the popular belief that people gain more maturity as they grow older. Overall, yes it is possible to improve your emotional quotient over the long term with intervention, guidance and regular practice.

Emotional Intelligence Be Developed

Our emotional intelligence pathway originates within the brain going right down to the spinal cord. The primary senses are involved here and must go to the brain's front portion before you start thinking logically or rationally about an occurrence. Emotions are generated in our limbic system, which is why our emotional response to an incident occurs before the rational mind gets involved. Emotional intelligence is based on efficient communication patterns between the brain's logical and emotional points.

Have you heard of plasticity? It is a term used by neurologists for describing the brain's ability to keep evolving and changing. The brain keeps growing newer connections as we acquire new skills. The change is slow, as the brain keeps developing more and more connections to boost its efficiency.

When you use various strategies for boosting emotional intelligence, you are actually letting the microscopic neurons (billions of them) lined between the emotional and logical centers of the brain to branch into smaller arms that touch other cells. This simply means, one cell can form more than 15,000 connections. The chain reaction signifies that it is simpler for the brain to adapt to this new behavior in the long term. Once the brain is trained with the help of emotional intelligence strategies, it becomes a habitual behavior/thought pattern.

Accurate Feedback

One of the most crucial aspects if you want to enhance your emotional quotient through any coaching intervention or self practice program is accurate feedback. People generally do not realize how others perceive them, especially people in senior management positions in organizations.

Though these folks are increasingly motivated, responsible and high on technical skills, they rarely take the time to pause and assess their behavior. In a nutshell, we do not possess a very accurate notion of how nice we come across as. Wishful thinking, misplaced optimism and overconfidence can be factors contributing to this blind spot.

Generally people tend to over evaluate themselves in the niceness department. They believe they are nicer than they actually are. Any effort at increasing your emotional quotient must begin with gaining a thorough understanding your strengths and weaknesses. Use valid and genuine assessment techniques like personality tests or accurate feedback to determine your success with developing a higher emotional quotient.

Some Methods Work More Efficiently Than Others

Some techniques for boosting emotional intelligence such as cognitive behavioral therapy for better psychological flexibility can work better than other methods. Since emotional intelligence is linked to human behavior, it can never be an exact science. The dynamics of human behavior, motivation, communication and feelings will keep changing. You have to identify and evaluate what works for you. While behavioral therapy works wonderfully well for some people, others may find meditation or deep breathing more effective in calming their emotions.

Here are some tried and tested tips for being the ultimate emotional intelligence ninja.

Respond Rather Than React

Reacting is a more unconscious and uncontrolled process that is a result of an emotional trigger. For instance, you snap when someone annoys you or you are already stressed due to another reason.

Responding, on the other hand, is more controlled and something you choose to do. You decide exactly how you behave in the given situation. For example, explaining to someone that you are not feeling too good and that this isn't the best time to interrupt you, and that later you'd be in a much better position to give them a good hearing. You've simply chosen to deal with the situation in a more productive and less impulsive manner by taking control of your emotions.

Evaluate how your actions will impact others before acting. If your behavior will affect others, try and place yourself in their shoes. How are they bound to feel if you say or do something? Would you like to go through the experience yourself? If you have to take a particular action, can you help people in coping with its effects?

Accept Responsibility for Your Feelings and Actions

This can be one of the most challenging yet productive tips for boost your emotional quotient. Your emotions originate from you and therefore you are completely responsible for them.

People around you may be responsible for creating certain situations but it is ultimately you who are in charge of your reaction to those situations. You may not always be able to control how others around you speak or behave. However, the way you react to their words and actions is something you have control over.

If you are hurt by someone and lash out, you are the one responsible for it. Get out of the mindset that "someone makes you do something." No one can make you angry; you are responsible for your anger. No one holds the strings to your emotions. No one makes you do or feel anything. Your reaction is completely your own responsibility. Your feelings can offer you important guidelines about your experience with different people along with your own requirements and preferences. However, your feelings and actions are no one's but your responsibility.

Once you start accepting responsibility for your feelings and behavior, it becomes simpler to manage it for impacting all spheres of your life positively.

If you hurt people, be gracious enough to accept it and apologize. Ignoring the person or not accepting the responsibility for your behavior is not a sign of high emotional intelligence. Your relationships will be much more positive and people will forgive you more easily if you make an honest attempt to set things right rather than live in denial land. Accepting your mistakes, apologizing and moving on is a sign of high emotional intelligence.

Be Assertive

Emotionally intelligent folks know the importance of setting appropriate boundaries to let people know our stand. You have the right to disagree with people without acting in a disagreeable manner. Learn to say refuse without feeling guilty when you are not up to something or you find people taking advantage of you. Set your priorities and safeguard yourself from stress, harm and duress.

Rather than using "you" followed by the accusation and putting people on the defensive foot, try making them more open to listening to and understanding your point. For instance, instead of saying "you should do this" or "you are xyx", try saying, "I feel really uncomfortable when you expect me to do this over my priorities" or "I strongly believe that I deserve recognition from the organization based on my consistent performance and contributions." See what we did there? We aren't putting people on the defensive by pointing a finger at them and saying, "you did this" or "you are like this." We are being assertive and talking about our feelings without blaming anybody.

Pay Close Attention to Your Behavior

You can only manage your emotions more effectively if you are consciously aware of it. It starts with paying very close attention to your emotions and their impact on your behavior. Emotional awareness is one of the cornerstones of EQ.

Start noticing how you act when you experience specific situations, and how it affects your everyday life. Do these feelings impact your productivity? How about your communication with other people? Do your emotions pose a threat to your overall well-being, including your physical and emotional health? How do you react when you are extremely angry, happy or sad? Once you are consciously aware of your reactions to emotions, you will be able to wield better control over them and channelize them more productively.

Practice Empathy

Empathy is all about trying to understand why someone feels or acts in the way they do by putting yourself in their shoes. It is also being able to communicate this understanding to them more effectively. Empathy can also apply to your emotions and feelings.

Each time you notice yourself experiencing a specific emotion or behavior, try and think why you feel the way you do. You may not be able to figure it out at the onset but pay close attention and you'll start receiving various answers that you didn't notice earlier.

When someone is experiencing a rather strong feeling, ask yourself how you would feel in a similar scenario. Always be interested in what people say to respond in a more sensitive manner.

It is always a good practice to ask questions and summarize what people say so you are clear, and people know you are actively listening to them.

When you put yourself in the other person's shoe, you reduce reactivity. For instance, if your child is resisting something you are telling him/her, try thinking it isn't easy for them to deal with peer pressure and academics. Think for a moment how it must be to be a young kid in the current competitive age.

 If your manager is being demanding and difficult, think about the pressure of performance expectation they are dealing with at the hands of senior management. When you start thinking more objectively by considering where the other person is coming from, understanding and conflict resolution become much simpler.

Managing other's emotions requires maturity, skill and tact. It starts by being aware of exactly where you want the person to go? Do you want to lead them to feeling happier, calmer, more aware, secure, vigilant or cautious, for instance? Once you realize how they are feeling and how to lead them there, you will know what to say and do.

We tend to forget how particular experiences feel; even we've lived through it ourselves. You can only imagine how much perspective limiting it becomes if we've not experienced what the other person is going through. What is the best way to bridge this gap? The nucleus of empathy lies in understanding the "why" among other things. Why does this person feel the way they do? What are they dealing with that I fail to see? Why do I experience different feelings than them? Explore your "whys" and you will be well on your way to better understanding the feelings of others.

Being kind, considerate and helpful is one of the best ways of practicing emotional intelligence.

Avoid Labeling Your Emotions

All your emotions are valid, including the not so positive ones. Avoid assigning labels and judging your emotions. When you judge your feelings, you inhibit your ability to experience them. When you cannot fully express or experience something, you prevent yourself from using these emotions more positively.

Each emotion you experience is a vital piece of information closely linked with what is happening around you and how it affects you. Without information about your emotions, you'd be left clueless about how to react to your emotions and manage them more effectively.

Connect negative feelings to events but avoid judging them to gain a better understanding. For instance, if you feel envious, try and figure out what the emotions is conveying to you about the situation. Learn to experience positive emotions so you recognize each opportunity to feel them to the fullest.

Practice Being More Light Hearted

When you are more light hearted and optimistic, it is simpler to capture the goodness of everyday situations and objects. Positivity results in greater emotional happiness and increased opportunities. People are forever looking to be around optimistic folks who come up with positive connections and possibilities. When you become more negative, you only concentrate on what can go awry rather than building strong resistance.

People with a more evolved emotional quotient know how to utilize wit and humor to make everyone feel happier, positive and safer. They know the art of using laugher to tide over tough times.

Use Your Mental Pause Button

Use your mental pause button each time you find yourself on the verge of speaking or acting. Take a moment, breathe deeply and think before you respond. Whenever you feel tempted to type an elaborate mail in rage, stop and think if it is going to help resolve the issue or only make it worse. Each time you feel like screaming at someone or making a combustible comment on the social media, apply the pause button.

When you consciously work on pausing before you speak or act, you get into the habit of thinking before acting or speaking in a manner that can worsen any situation. You learn to manage, control and tackle your emotions to handle any situation in a more constructive manner. When you learn to use this technique, you realize that the button to your feelings and emotions is in your hands.

When you sense a challenge in controlling impulses, deal with it by quickly diverting your attention. Distract your thoughts by counting or concentrating on a pre-planned diversion thought. Your mind can be trained to shift thoughts or conversations fast.

Practice Active Listening

During arguments or disagreements we often listen not to understand but to react and respond. When the other person is speaking, we are almost mentally constructing out own arguments to answer back or give back to them. This leads to even more conflict.

Dealing with conflict becomes more effective when you tackle issues in an assertive yet respective manner, without being defensive. When you listen empathetically, your own thoughts and emotions are taken into account. Listening actively and empathetically can help you shed toxic feelings building up in you.

Be assertive by all means, but also practice active listening to find that one point that can lead to resolution. Problem solution only happens when you understand where the other person is coming from and what they want. You can find a middle ground only when you tune in to the words, feelings and emotions of the other person, not just to give a fitting reply but also to resolve the issue. Listening is all about putting the other person's words, thoughts and feelings first.

Your opinion about people or events may not change. However, the time spent listening to the other person may just calm you and help you come up with a more positive or constructive response. It may help you see things from a different perspective and analyze the situation more objectively.

Be Open to Feedback

Boost your emotional intelligence by being more receptive to feedback. While you may disagree with the criticism/feedback, sometimes being open to other's views can help you identify behavior patterns that may be having an effect that you didn't intend. Healthy feedback can guard you from blind spots and adjust your behavior.

The more you exist in denial mode about destructive behavior, the more challenging it may be for you to develop a high emotional quotient. Acceptance and awareness is the key to increasing your emotional intelligence.

Practice Deep Breathing

Strong emotions impact us physically too. When we are stressed or anxious, our bodies respond in a more evolutionary instinctive manner like we're face to face with a nature based threat. The physical reactions include constricted blood vessels, shallow breathing and speedier heart rate.

When we learn to consciously manage our body's reaction to anxiety, the emotional attribute is lowered. Each time you feel nervous or tense, practice slow and deep breathing. Concentrate on the flow of the breath and the abdominal cavity. You will invariably feel better and calmer once you relax and create more space in your mind.

Mindfulness or mindful breathing is another way to achieve stillness of the mind by completely immersing yourself in the present non-judgmentally. When you get into the habit of identifying your thoughts and emotions with judgment, you boost your awareness and gain greater clarity rather than operating from a judgmental and assumption laden point of view. Mindfulness reduces your chances of being overtaken by negative or destructive emotions.

Decrease Negative Personalization

When we feel negatively impacted by someone's behavior, do not rush into a conclusion. Tempting as it is to ascribe a negative reason for their behavior, try to gather a more holistic perspective of the circumstances before reacting. For instance, it is easy to think a friend isn't returning your call or message because he/she wants to avoid you.

However, they may also be busy or ill or in a dire situation. When we avoid ascribing negative reasons or personalizing people's behavior, we view them more objectively and with less hateful/judgmental emotions. The ability to overcome negative personalization of people's behavior is critical for boosting your emotional quotient.

Develop Flexibility

Sometimes we get stuck in our own monotonous traps and become rigid and inflexible, which may impair our emotional intelligence. People with a highly developed emotional quotient know when to adapt and keep pace with newer techniques rather than getting stuck in an increasingly unproductive cycle. They know when how to adapt and manage their emotions according to the situation. Emotionally intelligent folks know when to adapt and shift perceptions.

Those who possess a highly developed emotional quotient are always open to newer experiences, challenging opportunities and a variety of adventures. Be open to change and shed the uneasiness and inhibitions attached with change.

Learn to decipher the consequences of your words and behavior. Emotionally intelligent folks pick their battles very selectively. They realize that peace and relationships are more valuable than being right.

When you learn to evaluate the consequences of your words and actions and demonstrate more flexibility and adaptability in your actions/words, you display high emotional intelligence. This isn't to be mistaken with letting people walk all over you. By all means, be assertive. However, know that it's not about being right or winning arguments all the time. Emotional intelligence is being perspective enough to realize what is worth fighting for and what is worth giving up.

Read Body Language

Try to gauge people's innermost emotions by tuning in to their body language. Pick up clues about their emotional health by observing their body language. Sometimes people say something while their expressions and gestures convey the opposite or a deeper truth they aren't comfortable revealing. When you practice being more mindful of their body language, you tap into their true emotional fabric to adapt you responses and reactions. Sometimes people resort to less conspicuous ways for communicating their emotions.

For instance, a person may try saying something reassuring but the high tone of their voice may defeat those words and indicate high stress. These are small yet powerful indicators of people's behavior patterns and reading them correctly will give you the power to unlock other's emotional framework.

Be Emotionally Honest

Be emotionally honest and transparent. You are not communicating genuinely if you shut yourself off from expressing emotions. If you say you are alright with a sorrowful face, you are being dishonest in your communication. When you practice being more real about emotions, it is easier for people to read it. It is always great to be able to be yourself and share your real feelings. It helps people know your feelings and understand where you are coming from. They trust you more, which sets the base for more rewarding relationships.

By all means manage your emotions so as to avoid hurting others but misleading others about your emotions or denying real deeper emotions is not a sign of high emotional intelligence.

Be Positive and Happy

How would you rate your happiness quotient on a scale of 1 to 10? Emotional intelligence originates from being happy and vice versa. They aren't simply happy because good things are happening to them but because they are great at managing and taking control of their own happiness.

Happiness originates from within. A person who is capable of managing his emotions efficiently wakes up joyfully each morning. These people encounter challenges too, just like everyone else. However, they do not let these issues dampen their zest for positivity. Develop greater emotional intelligence by keeping your mind clear, avoid getting caught in destructive self-pity and take charge of your happiness. Emotional intelligence comes with being more positive and solution oriented.

Happy people gain more appreciation and following from people to help them tide over tough times. They spread more happiness, live longer and come up with constructive solution. It is a misconception that happiness is a result of material possessions. Genuinely happy people are those who can manage their emotions well, spread happiness, and most importantly those who focus on giving rather than receiving. Emotionally intelligent people know that it costs zilch to be happy and yet the returns are invaluable.

Stop Complaining

One of the first steps towards boosting your emotional intelligence is to stop complaining. Shed the victim syndrome and know that the solution to your problem is well within your grasp. Emotionally intelligent people rarely blame others or their circumstances for the challenges in their life. Instead, they search for matured ways to dissolve a relationship or talk to people who've wronged them in private. They also have a steady stream of effective coping mechanisms such as yoga, meditation, nature trips or simply venting their feelings by writing.

Listen to Physical Clues

Some of the best indicators of our emotional condition are the physical signals our body gives us. You can develop a greater awareness of your emotions simply by tuning in to your physical sensations. You may feel a knot in your tummy while commuting to work, which can be a sign of high stress.

Similarly, when you are with someone you've recently started dating, and experience a too strong to ignore flutter in your heart, it could be an indication of having found the person who'd like to spend the rest of your life with. Our body is constantly trying to communicate emotions we may not be aware of through physical sensations. Listening to these feelings and emotions signaled by the body helps process our emotions and reactions more efficiently.

Tap Into Your Subconscious Mind

How can you gain a greater awareness of your subconscious emotions or feelings? Apart from deep breathing and mindfulness, let your thoughts wander freely and evaluate where they go. Pay close attention to your dreams. Are there any recurring symbols that can be closely connected with the current events in your life?

Keep a journal and pen next to your bed and write down the details you can recall about your most compelling dreams as soon as you are up. Analyze the emotions and patterns of these dreams, their symbolic references and the message they are trying to communicate. When you gain a thorough understanding of the emotions that dominate your subconscious mind, it becomes simpler to train your subconscious mind to guide your actions.

Sometimes, our conscious minds are unable to come with solutions we are faced with, which is why the phrase "sleep over it" originated. Our subconscious mind's functionality is at its peak when we are asleep. Ever wondered why many a times the solution to our problems strikes us when we are asleep? Or we wake up with a totally different perspective or solution much to our surprise? Our subconscious mind is ticking overtime when our conscious mind is resting. By tuning into our subconscious mind, we are tapping into our inner most emotional reserve to uncover our deepest feelings.

Resolve Conflicts Like a Boss

One of the best tips for developing high emotional quotient is mastering conflict management skills. Conflict resolution actually puts your emotional intelligence to practical use. Resolving differences and conflicts involves many aspects including identifying feelings, clear expression of thoughts, active listening, staying calm and coming up with a solution that diffuses the situation rather than escalating it. When we struggle to understand and control our feeling, we experience a sense of irritation, depression and erratic behavior patterns. Conflicts only get magnified, making it all the more stressful for to deal with. Once you recognize yours and other's emotions, and learn to manage them, you enjoy a happier and more balanced life.

Conclusion

Thank you for purchasing this book.

I hope the book was able to help you to understand the powerful concept of emotional intelligence and how you can use it in your everyday life to enjoy more rewarding personal and professional relationships.

There are lots of real life examples, actionable tips and practical pointers on how you can go about boosting your emotional quotient right away.

The next step is to simply take action and follow the proven techniques mentioned in the book.

Lastly, if you enjoyed reading the book, please take time to share your views with us by posting a review. It'd be highly appreciated!

Here's to your rewarding, enriching and emotionally healthy relationships!

Book #2
Empath

How to Thrive in Life as a Highly Sensitive-

The Ultimate Guide to Understanding and Embracing Your

Gift

Introduction

This is the Ultimate Guide for the Empath – basically, everything you need to know to understand what being an empath means and how you can embrace being one. It includes the following:

- What empaths are

- Theories about empaths and psychic abilities

- The traits and abilities of empaths

- How to tell whether someone is an empath or not

- Empath self-test

- The pros and cons of being an empath

- Common empath problems and how to solve them

- How to manage emotions

- How to consciously control empath abilities

- Psychic self-defense for empaths

- Psychic development for empaths

- Chakra development for empaths

- And more

If you are an empath or you know someone who is, reading this book and practicing the exercises mentioned here will go a long way into accepting the gift and maximizing its potential.

Although there are many books written about empaths, this book puts together all the valuable information and presents it in an easy-to-understand format so you can start applying them immediately.

Chapter 1.

Understanding Empaths and Empathy

An empath is someone who knows what another being feels, oftentimes by feeling it himself or herself. The ability of an empath is empathy. The word "empathy" is commonly understood the ability to share feelings with others, but it takes a whole new meaning when empaths are discussed.

Everyone has the ability to imagine being in another person's situation. However, a genuine empath can experience what another feels even if he or she does not observe anything from that person or has no idea about what he/she's going through. This is because it involves clairsentience (psychic feeling) and intuition (knowing something without relying on logic or reason).

In other words, an empath gains information about someone else's inner state through paranormal ways. Normal ways to know someone else's emotions are observing body language and guessing what a person feels based on his/her circumstances. An empath does not need to do these.

Aside from being able to know things through inexplicable ways, an empath will often be correct when he/she senses something. In contrast, someone who is not really an empath commonly makes wrong judgments. Thus, you can tell whether a person is really an empath or not by considering how many times he/she was right about something that was hard to know.

Empaths are highly perceptive so they make accurate conclusions. Despite this, they may have problems trusting their intuitions, especially when they grew up being told that their gut feelings were not true. But if they push aside what they know, their hunches may haunt them until they confirm that it's true all along. When others notice empaths do this, they turn to them to seek advice.

Empaths may also be capable of projecting energy and emotions to the environment, to those around them, or to a specific person. As you may imagine, this can tempt some to manipulate others, but more often than not, they would only use their abilities to help. Those who can sense and direct energy usually become healers who genuinely care about their patients.

As you may have noticed, empaths are extraordinary. This is why they are often misunderstood. If you think that you or someone you know is an empath, you will understand empathy better by learning about psychic abilities.

Theories about Psychic Ability

Empathy, the skill of empaths, is considered as one kind of psychic ability. There are some theories that explain how psychic abilities work:

Electromagnetic Theory

Some people used to think that information travels through space like electromagnetic waves. There are those who also claimed that consciousness itself is a form of electromagnetism. They believed that psychics can receive information and "thought waves" that are broadcasted by their sources.

The electromagnetic theory is not generally accepted nowadays because it does not explain how psychic information seems to travel faster than light (which is impossible for electromagnetic waves) and why it's still intact even when sent from far away (electromagnetic waves gradually dissipate the further they go). Researchers also found no evidence that the mind exists as a form of electromagnetism. However, this theory is not totally debunked; it just needs more evidence to be considered as true.

Psi Dimension Theory

The psi dimension theory assumes the existence of multiple dimensions, which some physicists and mathematicians say is possible. It states that there is a dimension where consciousness exists – some theorists call this the psi dimension (psi means psychic ability). This dimension is in another realm so it does not follow the laws of the universe we are in, but it is believed to intersect with this universe at some points. If this theory is correct, it explains why psychics can know things even if such things are far away from them or in the distant past/future.

Quantum Connection Theory

Quantum mechanics explores matter at the subatomic level, or at sizes that are smaller than the atom. At this level, matter behaves both like particles (solid stuff) and waves (energy), but it becomes a particle or wave based on what an observer decides to see.

This implies that consciousness has an effect on matter. When viewed at very high magnifications, matter can't be considered as real but only as a set of probabilities. As a consequence, researchers aren't sure if the existence of matter itself is real or imaginary at the core. To them, it seems as if consciousness somehow is involved in deciding whether things become real or not.

The quantum realm has laws that are so different from what we are used to that even those who have studied quantum mechanics are confused about them. For example, quantum entanglement gives particles the ability to affect one another even if they are miles apart from each other. This lead to a theory that everything is connected at the quantum level especially because everything came from one source (many scientists consider this origin as the Big Bang).

Some parapsychologists (psychic ability researchers) and consciousness researchers believe that the mind itself is a quantum phenomenon. They say that people can gather and send information via quantum entanglement of their minds with others' minds and with everything else. This is also a possible explanation for why some people can affect other people's minds and manifest a particular kind of reality.

So far, these are just guesses about how psychic abilities can exist. What is sure is that there are people who have them – such as the empaths.

Theories about Empaths

Empaths in particular are said to be the way they are because of the following:

Weak Boundaries

It is believed that emotions radiate from sources into the area around them. Empaths easily pick these emanations because their systems are calibrated to receive them, or because their boundaries are weaker than other people. In contrast, non-empaths are "dense" and preoccupied with their own thoughts and emotions. They may also have a stronger energetic shield around them that blocks subtle vibrations from entering their awareness.

Sensitive Auric Field

Empaths may have a high degree of sensitivity to what's inside their aura, which some say is the extension of the soul. Thus, if others' energies manage to enter their auric field, they will likewise feel it. This may also explain why they are sensitive to sensory stimuli.

Active chakras

Chakras are energy portals along the spine. Some believe that empaths have hyperactive chakras so they can perceive and release energies more readily. On the other hand, an empath is also in danger of depleted chakras because their personal energy tends to get drained easily (you'll learn why later).

Energy Links

Empaths may unintentionally form cords or energy links to those around them. This causes them to receive more input than others. Sometimes, they may do this with full awareness because they want to understand and sympathize. For them, being connected is just a natural way of life, and they don't really consider themselves as separate from those around them.

Traits of an Empath

An empath is sometimes considered as a highly sensitive person (HSP). This is partially true because being an HSP means being more sensitive to stimuli than most people. However, an empath's traits go far beyond hypersensitivity. Before discussing these, here is a test to confirm whether you are an empath or not.

Self-Test for Empaths

Answer the questions with a yes or no. Don't spend too much time on each number; just go with your automatic response.

- Are you easily overwhelmed? [Yes/No]

- Are you intolerant of noisy, chaotic environments? [Yes/No]

- Are you distressed by bright lights, strong smells, coarse fabrics, or loud sounds? [Yes/No]

- Do you get startled a lot? [Yes/No]

- Do you notice small changes around you or in other people quite easily? [Yes/No]

- Do you think that you have an extra-sensitive nervous system? [Yes/No]

- Do you easily detect whenever someone experiences a change of mood? [Yes/No]

- Do you constantly worry about how others feel? [Yes/No]

- Do other people's moods affect you a lot? [Yes/No]

- Do you find yourself reflecting on things that others don't usually think about? [Yes/No]

- Are you conscientious? [Yes/No]

- When you are with others, do you know what to do to make others more comfortable? [Yes/No]

- Do you often crave to be alone after being with a lot of people? [Yes/No]

- Do you listen to your heart more than your head? [Yes/No]

- Do you cry easily? [Yes/No]

- Do you avoid violent, scary, or depressing shows? [Yes/No]

- Do you favor pleasant music, works of arts, scenes, tastes, scents, etc? [Yes/No]

- When you were young, did your parents or teacher describe you as sensitive or shy? [Yes/No]

- Do you plan your activities so you avoid situations that may upset you or anyone else? [Yes/No]

- Do you find it hard to be observed while you are doing something? [Yes/No]

- Are you highly aware of details and subtleties? [Yes/No]

- Do you frequently experience strong emotions? [Yes/No]

- Do you dislike confrontations immensely? [Yes/No]

- Are you told not to be too sensitive? [Yes/No]

- Do you find it difficult to say no? [Yes/No]

- Do you often not say what you mean to avoid offending someone? [Yes/No]

- Do you notice mistakes faster than most people? [Yes/No]

- Are you quick to notice who is not being nice to others? [Yes/No]

- Do you prefer doing things alone? [Yes/No]

- Are you indecisive? [Yes/No]

- Are you a perfectionist? [Yes/No]

- Do you like thought provoking questions? [Yes/No]

- Do you know someone's emotional state without knowing why? [Yes/No]

- Do you feel energy coming from or being drained by someone or something? [Yes/No]

- Do you sense danger reliably? [Yes/No]

- Have you avoided harmful situations based on your gut feel? [Yes/No]

- Are you drawn to nature? [Yes/No]

- Do you love animals? [Yes/No]

- Do you feel others' pain as if it was your own? [Yes/No]

- Do you have a bigger perspective than others you know? [Yes/No]

- Do you hate crowds? [Yes/No]

All Yes answers count as an empath trait. The more you have, the more likely it is that you're an empath.

Living Life as an Empath

As mentioned, empaths are sometimes labeled as hypersensitive persons, but not all HSPs are empaths. They are similar to HSPs because they can be highly sensitive to sensory or emotional input. The main thing that differentiates empaths from others is their ability to gain information about somebody else's emotional state without relying on normal cues.

What distinguishes empaths from other psychics is that they are emotionally centered. They feel emotions more intensely, thus they are more responsive to emotions as well. When making decisions, they usually follow their heart, however, when they made mistakes, they tend to feel so bad about it that they may develop perfectionism.

Empaths are more than just emotional people – they literally absorb emotions of those near them. Sometimes, they can also perceive feelings of people who are far away when they unintentionally connect to them. When this happens, it can be confusing for empaths because there is nothing in the environment to explain why they are feeling the way they do.

Empaths need to distinguish their own feelings from others. They must develop a higher degree of self-awareness so they would not be overwhelmed by what they feel. When they learn how to do this, they can take advantage of their gift to learn what they need to know without being swept of their feet.

Empaths are highly intuitive and has a deep desire to understand. They have sharper than normal observation skills that enable them to comprehend things more. This also makes them more understanding of other people, thus they can be good counselors and healers. They can step into another person's shoes to gain a more balanced, more complete view of something. Others would go beyond knowing what a person feels but pinpoint the emotion's cause. They do this because they can easily sense whenever there are things going on beneath the surface. Because of this, they can be quite smart, and it is quite difficult to lie to an empath especially those who can read minds as well.

Empaths are often smart. They are curious about a lot of things and view diverse issues with an open mind. This makes them learn more than those that have a lot of biases. Sometimes, they would use their abilities to know more about a person and why he/she thinks that way so they can communicate better. There are also those who will telepathically link to someone else who knows a lot about the thing they are interested in – eventually, they become experts themselves.

They can provide valuable input because they can analyze well, calculate the pros and cons, and see one thing from various perspectives, but they need to be helped by someone else who are good with making decisions. They take a longer time to make decisions because they mind things that others ignore, such as the effect of their choice upon others and the possible outcomes.

Empaths are conscientious. They have concern over how others will be reacting. Thus, they are polite, well-mannered, and have likeable personalities. They are also likely to notice when someone else is not being conscientious.

Empaths have a greater sense of responsibility and justice. They can feel whenever people are wronged or in distress so they tend to become protectors. Unlike many people, empaths care about more things aside their personal interests. They strive to help others, even if they would not receive any direct benefit from doing so.

Empaths can't stand horror or violence even if fictional because of their empathy and emotional sensitivity. They cry more easily even from just watching a dramatic TV show. Because they can be emotional, they need to be in situations where they can cry or express what they feel without being embarrassed or scolded.

Shyness among empaths may be caused by two things: being more sensitive and being different. Empaths can easily know what people really think about them even if they don't say anything. This can make them become self-conscious. Also, being unique can make them feel as if they don't belong. Sometimes, people tease them for not acting like everybody else, so they learn to keep things to themselves to avoid being ridiculed. This shyness is usually overcome as the empath learns that it's okay to be who he/she is.

Although one common trait among empaths is that they are shy, they can be extroverts as well. Empaths can be good team players because they think deeply and care about other members. They attract people who talk to them because they are good listeners. A lot ask for their advice because they understand people and their emotions.

Empaths can make people reflect upon themselves. Since empaths can feel others emotions (and sometimes thoughts) as if they are their own, they can talk about what's going on in a person's consciousness. Sometimes, they can read a person like an open book. When they tell what they can pick up from another person, he or she can self-reflect better.

Empaths are generally understanding of other people and their situations. They do not usually judge others because they can easily put themselves in their place, and they know the reasons why people are the way they are. Other than this, they tend to please people. They are friends with everyone and do not take sides. This may not be welcomed by some kinds of people though, and they can be misunderstood as being traitors or inauthentic.

Empaths sometimes have trouble knowing who they really are, because they have an intuitive sense of connection with everything and everyone around them. They take on others' joys and burdens easily as if they are one with them. When others are in trouble, they easily sympathize and find ways to help them. This makes them vulnerable to those who take advantage of their good nature. When this happens, they can be overly defensive and shut themselves off from others.

Empaths like to improve things. Many empaths are driven to create positive changes. Their inborn creativity, imagination, and resourcefulness help them to accomplish these. This is because they easily notice whenever something is wrong or there is something that is lacking. They want to help the needy and make life better for them.

Empaths are passionate. When empaths find something they care about, they pour all their heart to it. When they are taken away from their interests, they may become heart-broken.

Empaths can be burdened. When empaths do not understand their condition, they become overwhelmed. They may think that there's something wrong with them – this can make them feel depressed to the point of being suicidal. They may choose to be alone and avoid social interaction, causing them to be more misunderstood. Some escape their emotions by drinking too much or taking drugs. However, if they manage to handle their situation, they can gain immense inner strength that enables them to help everyone they encounter.

Empaths can lash out. Empaths are usually gentle creatures because of their natural ability to feel others' pain. There are times though that they can take in too much negativity that they can't help but release some of it. More often, they would choose to remove themselves so they would not harm anyone and they won't have to absorb more than they could take.

Empaths are often selfless. Sometimes, they are more aware of others' feelings more than their own. This makes them become less self-centered and more oriented towards others' wellbeing.

They also have e need to take care of those around them. They are good listeners and can be very insightful counselors.

However, empaths can be narcissistic too. Although empaths are one of those who are more perceptive of others, they can sometimes fight against what they feel by developing narcissism. They may consider their gift as something that makes them more special than others. Doing this makes them feel more in control despite being greatly affected by those around them. They can also be more selfish because they feel as if others are draining them too much and they have to protect what is theirs.

On the other hand, narcissists can seem like empaths because of their ability to read people. The important difference between the two is that an empath tries to understand others to help them, while a narcissist does so to take advantage of them.

Although narcissists may seem thick-skinned, they are in fact vulnerable like the empaths. They only pretend that they are tough while empaths do not. Also, narcissists harm others when they are harmed. Empaths do not. They will change themselves to make their relationships more harmonious. Narcissists will just force everyone to be more agreeable to them.

The defining characteristic of narcissists is their overinflated egos. This is unusual among empaths because they consider themselves as equal to others. While narcissists do not hesitate stepping upon other people to get ahead in life, empaths will often consider how their actions affect others.

Narcissists may be sensitive to feelings like empaths, but while empaths will extend compassion, narcissists will be hostile when they experience others' discomfort. They do not bother to understand others' emotions but instead focus on ways to make themselves feel superior.

There are those who consider empaths and narcissists as polar opposites, but many empaths can be empathic or narcissistic depending on the situation. Don't feel guilty if you think you are being narcissistic sometimes. It's possible that you are just protecting yourself from being drained that's why you became more self-centered than you usually are.

So, how did your test go? Did you recognize yourself or someone you know in the traits described above? The next part will explain just what the empath can do. After finishing this book, you will know how to maximize abilities that only empaths are gifted with.

Manifestations of Empath Abilities

Empaths manifest their abilities differently. There are those who intellectually know others' emotions while others feel the same thing. Some empaths sense emotions as a physical sensation – like heat, cold, electric shocks, and the like.

Many empaths pick up what another is feeling by being near that person. Some empaths are more sensitive to certain kinds of people because they are more receptive to them or can relate to them in some way. There are also empaths who can connect to animals or plants; sometimes, more than other humans.

Other empaths sense emotions in the air, such as in places where strong emotions were discharged. There are those who switch to another person's perspective when they watch the news, read something, touch someone's belongings, or simply think about someone.

Empaths' traits may change depending on a variety of factors, such as their own emotions, state of mind, relationship with others, and more. Thus, an empath can have varying experiences. However, an empath can learn to bring his/her abilities under conscious control to make his/her experiences more consistent.

Empaths can connect with others emotionally and intellectually. Emotionally, an empath may physically feel the emotions and subtle energies of others. This makes them more attuned to another's internal states. Intellectually, an empath may imagine himself or herself in somebody's place to understand the other more. This makes them more able to understand the other's perceptions, thoughts, and beliefs.

Some empaths have an ability to affect other people's realities because they can connect deeply. They can also have healing abilities because they can see energy and send healing energy towards where it is needed. Healer empaths may sometimes feel another's pain, but unlike the other person, he or she may know what to do to heal it.

Spiritual empaths may sense other people's connection to their god/s. They may help others to have a deeper spirituality as well. These people may eventually become spiritual leaders or members of the clergy.

Empaths may be precognitive and can predict other people's futures. They can become reliable oracle readers. But take note that not all fortunetellers are empaths. If one is an empath as well, he/she can read better because he/she will be able to sense information about the client that is missed by a reader who is not an empath.

There are empaths who connect more to animals and nature more than people. They can be excellent animal whisperers or gardeners. Some environmentalists and animal rights activists may be empaths.

Now that you understand empaths more fully, let's go to the next part of the book: trouble-shooting empath problems.

Chapter 2.

Empath-Related Problems and How to Overcome Them

Having empath abilities gives a person an interesting life. It turns a person into a superhero of a sort, but at the same time presents challenges that don't afflict non-empaths.

It may be tempting to give away these cursed "superpowers" to somebody else. Unfortunately, not only is it impossible, but rejecting them does not really help anyone. The first step towards coping is to acknowledge that you are an empath and to look at your situation objectively.

Pros and Cons of Being an Empath

Being an empath is not so bad; you just have to deal with some issues. Empathy is the ability to connect to a person at a deep level. This enables the empath to know what another is truly feeling even though he/she may be hiding or disguising it. This kind of understanding is valuable for those whose work involves relating to people, such as social workers, teachers, coaches, counselors, psychologists, nurses, therapists, managers, administrators, lawyers, detectives, salespeople, clergy, and the likes.

Empaths can potentially develop better relationships and solve problems because they can understand what people really feel. They can see through others' eyes instead of being stuck on their own perspectives. They feel the dynamics of a relationship so they know why things are how they are. Because they notice more than the average person, they may communicate better, be more influential, and fix more things.

There are downsides to this, though. There are some tasks and situations that need objectivity and not emotionality – empaths may have problems handling these. Making tough decisions that have a negative on impact on others is one of them.

Extra-sensitive empaths may be overwhelmed by the things they pick up. Because of the extra information, they may become indecisive and prone to mood swings. When they are regularly subjected to unpleasant or overstimulating moods, their physical and psychological health may suffer.

When they feel other people's pain intensely, they may suffer themselves and be unable to help. This frustrates them so much because they feel powerless, they feel guilty because they can't do anything, and they also feel the other party's misery of not receiving any help. Because of this, empaths are encouraged to choose who to help, detach themselves from those they are helping so they can actually do something instead of be carried away by intense emotions.

Empaths may seek relief by escaping social situations and being alone, which they will benefit greatly from. Unfortunately, those who are close to them may not understand this need so they will prevent the empath from running away from them. Aside from this, they are judged harshly by society, especially one that does not know about empathy and other psychic traits. Sometimes, they numb the intensity of what they feel through mind-altering substances such as liquor and drugs – these may help temporarily but ultimately leave them in worse conditions.

The high sensitivity of empaths makes them catch what most people will miss. On the downside, they may become overwhelmed easily. Unless they find ways to manage how they respond to information and stimuli, they might become nervous wrecks and recluses.

Sometimes, empaths may be good mediums and clairvoyants. This makes them interesting to the spirit world. Because of this, they may attract both good and bad spirits. Unfortunately, some of these spirits may feed off on their energies because they have weak boundaries and they emit energies strongly.

In conclusion, being an empath gives one gifts and burdens. By learning to master the ability, you can use it to your advantage and lessen its inconveniences. The following chapters will deal with each issue thoroughly.

Chapter 3.

Psychic Self-Defense for Empaths

Empaths need to protect themselves because they can be sensitive to energies and entities that do not usually bother those who are not empaths or psychics. This chapter is about psychic self-defense measures. This is useful especially to those who are into the occult as well.

A disclaimer: the measures given in this chapter are fairly easy to do and won't take much time, but these may or may not work depending on what's actually happening.

When something's bothering you, investigate what's involved: are you having health issues? Do you need to talk with a counselor? Are you doing some things that are causing you harm? It's easy to confuse normal issues with paranormal ones. For best results, only use these measures as support. Get to the root cause of your problem and do something about it.

Shielding

Empaths are sometimes clairvoyant as well and can see subtle energies that are normally invisible. Whether you see energy or not, you can direct it with your will and imagination.

Shields are an example of things you can create out of your thoughts. You can use them to filter out unwanted emotions and vibes from other people. You may create a shield for several purposes:

- To increase your sense of security

- To reduce the level of stimulation that reaches you

- To ward off attacks

- To make yourself less noticeable to psychic vampires and black magicians

- To avoid being overwhelmed by emotions

An empath's aura has an outer layer that is thinner than those who are not empaths. It may have holes in it as well, thus the person is more easily influenced by other people and things in the environment.

These are some things that can weaken your auric shield:

- Injuries

- Trauma

- Addictions

- Extreme emotions

- Permissions

To keep your shield intact, take care of your physical and psychological health. Meditate regularly to preserve your inner peace. Avoid giving permission to anyone or anything to ruin your auric shield.

Imagine a shield made of light and energy around your body. Visualize it as bright, clear, and solid. When you make a shield, you may clairvoyantly see it as having a particular color. You can keep this color or change it to something else. Good colors to use are gold or white. However, you can use your own color for as long as it represents protection for you.

Caution: some of those who use shields have reported that a shield only lasts for around 4 hours because it dissipates into the environment. Reconstruct your shield after 4 hours or when you feel its effects wear off.

Another thing you must remember is that you don't need to have a shield around with you at all times. If you want to connect with other people more, or if you want to feel something better, you can literally "lower your shields" to let in the energy. It's also perfectly fine not to use shields when you don't feel the need to have one up.

Get Help from a Friend

A friend can act as a living buffer of energy. If you feel as if you can't cope with the energies in a place or situation, ask a friend to stay next to you. His/her own aura may compensate for yours for the meantime. Interacting with another person can also distract you from whatever you're feeling.

Protective Tools

These are some physical items that are commonly used as psychic self-defense tools:

Mirror

A mirror is useful for deflecting negativity, especially when psychic attacks are intentionally directed to you. Get a small mirror and keep it in a pocket or wear it as a pendant with the reflective side facing away from your body. Intend that it will deflect attacks or unwanted energies aimed towards your person. Take note that this may work even if the person does not intentionally mean you harm, so use this only if you're sure that you won't be harming anyone you care about. The advantage of this technique is that you don't use your own energy to deflect attacks.

Crystals

Crystals can help absorb negative energies and give you protection and empowerment. Because they contain energy and have a sort of intelligence of their own, you can program them to perform simple functions such as disintegrating negative thought forms, alerting you of danger, deflecting harmful vibes, and the like.

A clear quartz crystal is an all-around amplifier of energy. You can program it to give you strength especially at times when you feel drained. To program, just talk to it in your mind or aloud and tell it what to do. If you think you have problems with a particular chakra (see chapter 5: chakra development), get a crystal that corresponds to that chakra.

You can also choose any crystal that you feel good holding. You don't have to follow the suggestions given in this book because they may have different effects on people. What's important is that you choose something that actually helps you.

Crystals have varying effects on empaths. There are many uses for crystals, but ultimately, you can program any crystal to do a specific function. However, there are some that are recommended for empaths because they are believed to have beneficial effects to them:

Quartz in general is an energy amplifier. Rose quartz in particular emanates love, so you can use it to counteract negative moods. Smoky quartz is a protection stone because it draws in negative energy and transmutes it into a pure form. It also helps with grounding.

Amber and black tourmaline absorbs negative energy. Having these stones will help lessen the negativities that your aura soaks up. You have to clean these crystals regularly though – if they get saturated, the energies may leak into the environment.

Onyx and black obsidian repel negative energy. The advantage of these is that they do not keep the bad energy, but they may launch it to someone accidentally. To prevent mishaps, instruct the crystal to transmute the energy into a positive form before deflecting it.

Red gemstones such as rubies, red jasper, and garnet tap into the root chakra and strengthen your sense of security.

Read more about crystals so you will have an idea of what may be best for your particular situation. Experiment with them by keeping it with you for about a week. Afterwards, look back and review what happened.

Salt Water

Water is an absorber of energy and salt is a purifier. If you feel psychically unclean, soak in a bath tub with salt water. You can also put it in a bowl and keep it near you. Just mix rock salt with clean water, preferably obtained from a natural source.

Cactus

A cactus can be programmed to destroy negative energy and thought forms in a place. It is said to emanate sharp energy needles that can puncture and disintegrate these unwanted vibes. Take care of the plant to show your appreciation for its help.

Amulets

You may wear an amulet or charm to protect yourself from energy vampires, psychic attacks, negative energies, and the like. These are available in occult shops. You can also turn any accessory into one. Just program it with your intention by saying it aloud or in your mind then charging it with energy (through visualizing energy entering it or by letting it soak the sunlight or moonlight).

Food

The food you eat may have greater effects on you if you're an empath since you react not only to its physical components but its energetic components as well. Thus, choose what you eat. It's better if the food is prepared humanely – slaughtered animals will leave food that is contaminated with negative emotions. You don't need to be vegetarian but it will greatly help decrease the amount of negative energies you consume. Eat healthy, stay away from junk and processed food, and drink a lot of clean water to keep yourself clean physically and energetically.

If it's hard for you to control your diet, try to bless your food at least. This will help erase the negativities you consume and imbue it with life-giving energies. Blessing can be in the form of a prayer, a request for the Divine to cleanse it, or a visualization of energy.

Avoiding Psychically Unclean People

People with a lot of issues may sometimes develop a tendency to emit unhealthy energies or deplete the energy of those around them. As an empath, you will be more vulnerable to these individuals. You may even have difficulty standing next to them or interacting with them over the phone or online. Do not spend a lot of time with them (whether physically or otherwise – energy can travel through connections) because it will be quite easy for them to penetrate your aura and feed off your vital energy since you already have a thin auric shield. If you can't avoid the person, protect yourself. Don't think that you are being heroic because you are "helping" the other person even if you end up depleted.

When these kinds of people give you something or touch your items, cleanse it. They may leave some energy residues or even thought forms or entities that will continue to deplete you even if they're not around. You will read more about cleansing later.

Dealing with Negative Entities

There are spirit entities that may become attracted to an empath because he/she has thin barriers, reacts strongly to stimuli, and can influence other people. Thus, they can attach themselves to the aura to leech off their energy and control them so they behave in ways that makes them generate more energy.

These entities may do this for varying reasons – one is to feed off energy by making the empath respond a certain way and another is to stop the empath from helping other people so they stop emitting negative vibrations, since empaths tend to help others become more positive.

As an example, there are entities that thrive on the emotional energy of anger. To acquire this energy, they inject thoughts and influence situations so that a person becomes angry. When they succeed, they will gather the energies that are generated. The more people affected, the bigger their meal.

Because of this, they will try to stop an empath or someone who is preventing the energies from being generated. Some say that this is one reason why empaths are prone to being distressed – some entities are deliberately making them feel this way to hinder their efforts to help people.

It's easy to become angry at these parasitic entities for unfairly getting something that is not theirs and causing harm to you. However, you must know that you must not attack them because that will only give them more of the same energy they are trying to harvest from you. Being negative towards them will just boost their negativity and make them more capable of doing you harm.

Instead, send them the opposite of their energy. Bless them. Understand that they are just doing that because they just want to survive. Currently, they can't get energy from the Universe because they are not evolved enough. Sending them love and positivity may help them evolve so they would no longer resort to parasitic means to be okay.

Getting angry or fearful of them will just form cords that they can exploit. Forgiveness helps remove these unhealthy attachments. After all, we eat other beings to live, too.

From time to time, and especially when you seem drained or influenced by these creatures, cleanse your aura by emanating light from the center of your beings. Let this radiate outwards and imagine the beings falling away from your aura. Accompany this with emotions of love and serenity. Fill your mind with the most joyful and loving thoughts. Do not allow any negative sentiment to creep in to prevent these entities to hang on.

Remember that the spirit is indestructible and they can only be transformed. So don't think about harming or killing other spirit beings – it's impossible and doing so will just bring up feelings of hostility. Help them help themselves, instead. Raise their vibrations so they will no longer need to be parasitic. At the very least, radiating energy that is contrary to these beings' nature will make them leave you.

Cording

People create energetic links to one another. Clairvoyantly, they can be seen as actual cords – some of them very thin while others are thick and composed of many cords interwoven together. The more energy involved, the bigger the cords are. These cords enable energy to flow to and from the chakras of the people involved.

Symptoms of Cords

You will know that you have formed cords when you experience one or more of these:

- Obsessive thoughts

- Inability to let go

- Frequent conversations/arguments in your mind with someone

- Constantly remembering the person

- Being tempted to go back to an old, unhealthy relationship

- Stalking

- Negative feelings about past

- Wanting to take revenge

- Crying so much

- Disinterest in other people

Why Cut Cords

Cutting cords may seem like a drastic measure especially if you've grown fond of the person or object, but consider these benefits:

- To attain peace of mind

- To think more clearly

- To prevent being manipulated

- To increase freedom

- To be relieved of burdens

- To move on

- To avoid being depleted

- To stop hurting another

- To regain your energy

- To make the other person/being become independent

Who to cut cords with

You don't need to cut cords with people whom you genuinely care about and who feel the same way for you. For as long as the relationship is healthy and everyone is benefitting, the cords will help. Otherwise, severe cords with:

- Those who you're obsessed with

- Those who have bothered you

- Those who have abused you

- Those who you have abused

- Those you're attached/dependent to

- Those who you think are holding you back in some way

How to Cut Cords

You may call upon spirit guardians to help remove cords from your aura. Although the guides can remove cords and attachments without being instructed to, they usually respect your free will and will only do so when you ask them to.

You can try this prayer or create something similar:

"I ask my guides to help remove cords that bind me to (name of person)."

If you don't know who is attached to you in particular, just request that all unhelpful cords will be severed.

You can also ask that the energy that is taken from you will be given back, or unwelcome energy be sent back to the owner. If you don't want to harm the person, ask that the energy be converted into a beneficial form before it is sent to the origin. Remember, attacking tends to make things worse so seek a resolution instead.

When you have removed all attachments through visualization and changing your attitude, forgive the person/creature with all your heart. This may be difficult to do, but once you managed to, you can be assured that you have totally released the attachment and would not unintentionally send cords to the subject.

Reflect on the relationship. What lessons have you learned? Take this to heart and let it change you into a better person. Show gratitude for the lessons and affirm that the connection is no longer necessary. This will allow both of you to move on and learn new lessons.

Processing the relationship and letting go may release some toxic energies so you need to clean up afterwards. Relax your body and clear your mind of troublesome thoughts. Imagine a white or golden light sweeping your aura until it becomes clean and radiant.

When you are already satisfied with how your aura looks and feels, seal it off. Imagine fortifying the boundary of your aura so all holes, tears, and cracks are closed off. Affirm that your aura will let only positive energy in and let out negative energy.

Cleansing the Aura

An empath draws in energy from the environment to the point that he/she becomes saturated with all sorts of emotions and vibes. Because of this, it's recommended to practice regular cleansing of the absorbed energy.

Another way of aura cleansing aside from visualizing light is to create a connection with the earth so that you can "dump" the toxic energy in there. Don't worry that you will hurt the earth because the planet is big enough to handle it. It also has the ability to transform negative energy into positive just like it turns dead material into living organisms.

There are many other ways of clearing the energy, such as:

- Reiki

- Tai Chi/Qi Gong

- Meditation

- Psychotherapy

- Resolving issues

- Lifestyle changes

The main point of energy clearing is removing yourself of negative emotions. If you feel better and you think more clearly, it is a symptom that you have cleared your energy.

Replenishing Energy

Clearing out your aura can leave you drained so always replace the old, dirty energy with fresh, clean energy. It's better if you do this in an environment that has little pollution and a lot of plant life. You can also tap into the energy of the sun for this. Let the sun rays remove your unclean energy and at the same time give you new vitality. As much as possible, keep yourself healthy so you will have maximum access to energy.

Grounding

Grounding reconnects you to the strength and stability of the earth. This will make you less vulnerable to energetic influences. After working with energy, you must ground yourself so you will not feel light-headed and out of touch with reality.

A simple way to ground yourself is to eat something light. Walking barefoot or doing something physical is also recommended. For more grounding ideas, go to Chapter 5 and look for the section on the Root Chakra.

A more effective yet more challenging way to feel grounded is to resolve your issues. Anything that is left unresolved will make you feel uneasy until you come into terms with it. Once you do, though, you won't have to rely on superficial and temporary means to achieve stability.

Don't worry if you haven't completely resolved your problems yet, though. Just immerse yourself in something that you enjoy. Be with people you like. This should give you a feeling that you are safe and welcome – a sign that you have sufficiently grounded yourself.

Vacationing into Nature

Cities are filled with emotions that may overwhelm an empath. Going away from the city and staying in a place without much people will help the empath regain his/her stability. Nature does contain plants and animals that also have their own version of emotions, but these are often not intense as humans'. Plants are said to radiate a calming energy as well. When you or an empath you know is overloaded, go away from crowds and spend a few hours in a secluded nature spot. You can tap into the energy of nature to replenish yourself.

Clearing Negative Energy from Your Surroundings

Because you are more sensitive to energy, you will know easily whether a place or an environment will be good to you. The downside is that you will be affected by things that don't matter to others. For this, you need to clean the energy of your environment. This can be done through a lot of ways:

Visualization

Energy follows thought – this means that whatever you think and imagine will carry energy that will follow your instruction. Remove all thoughts from your mind for as much as you could. With eyes closed, intend to see the area within your mind's eye.

At this point, you may have an intuition of what to do. A spirit guide may also come in and give some instructions. If not, you can simply imagine negativities to be darkness, clouds, or whatever represents unclean energy to you. Visualize clearing these out with radiant light, a gentle breeze, purifying fire, or whatever cleansing method you want.

Smudging with Incense

Incense has long been used to purify a place. It will also leave the room smelling good, which will improve people's moods. Go with incense that appeals with you. Some suggestions are frankincense (traditionally used for purification), lavender (has calming properties), and sage (often used for mystic rituals).

Using Sound

Sound waves can push away unclean energies and entities from an area. Ringing a bell, chime, or singing bowl will emit a pure vibration that will repel anything that is impure. If you don't have these instruments, you may chant a mantra or play music that makes you feel peaceful and happy. In fact, some have played Disney songs to remove negative spirits from houses! Don't worry too much about the right song to play though. Anything will work for so long as it puts you in a pleasant state when you hear it.

Placing Bowls of Rock Salt on Crucial Areas

Rock salt has long been used for discouraging evil spirits from entering an area and for cleansing things or people that are believed to be contaminated by undesirable energy. Use rock salt because table salt is already processed and subjected to artificial chemicals and forces. The more natural the salt you get, the more charged with energy it is.

Put the bowls in areas where you sense something off. The doorway is a good spot because it will filter everyone and everything that passes through it. Another good area is underneath your bed as the negative energy you have accumulated during the day will be cleansed as you sleep.

Program the bowls with your intention. Imbuing it with your thoughts will make it more effective. Change the salt at least once a week to remove the dirty energy collected.

Physically Clean the Place

Physical things have an energetic counterpart. Cleaning the place not only makes it more comfortable and safe at the superficial level, it also improves its energetic quality. Because entities are attracted to energy that is similar to them, if your place is dirty, you may unknowingly invite dirty spirits too. Also, the condition of your place has effects on people around you, so make it easy for people to feel good by tidying up.

These should take care of most issues that deal with energies and entities. If you still need help, consider hiring a reliable psychic/mystic/occultist. Read reviews first so you know what to expect!

Chapter 4.

Consciously Controlling Empath Abilities

Being more familiar with empath skills will help you use it to your advantage rather than be knocked off every time the abilities kick in without your consent. Before anything, recall the times when you have manifested some form of empath ability. What happened? How did it feel like? What did you do? Recall as many details as you can and record these in a journal. When you pay more attention to your experiences, you will be more ready to control them.

As an empath, you may have sent and received emotions and other psychic information without intending to. This time, you will do so deliberately. Before doing these exercises, you need to clear your mind of all thoughts and calm down all emotions. This will lead to more accurate results. Record everything that happens as well.

Sending and Receiving Emotions

Normally, emotions are easy telepathy targets because the subconscious mind (the psychic part of the mind) deals with emotions. As an empath, you will be more adept in receiving and interpreting feelings.

To hone your natural gift, you may practice deliberately sensing emotion with a partner. You may take turns being the sender and receiver of emotion.

The sender will spend some minutes in generating a strong feeling in himself or herself. This can be done by recalling experiences when the emotion occurred, imagining scenarios that provoke the feeling, or by visualizing concepts associated with it (example, darkness, scary noises, and running people can be linked with fear). The receiver will clear his/her mind and heart and wait until he/she feels something else. To help with the connection, the sender and receiver may imagine a tube connecting their hearts. The receiver will say what he/she received and guess the emotion.

Sending Emotions

Imagine your target. Feel his or her presence with your mind and being. Look at the target. If not present, pretend that he or she is in front of you. If you are targeting a group, see them around you. Have the intention of connecting with the target/s.

Pick an emotion and make yourself feel it. Bring back memories or think of thoughts that will evoke the feeling. Let it fill your awareness.

When it has reached its peak strength and concentration, pass it on to your target/s. Ask the person or the group if they felt something and what particular emotion they experienced. Intensify the emotion, re-establish the connection, and send it again if they got the wrong result or if they did not feel anything.

When you're done, relax and ground yourself. Release all emotional energy.

Receiving Emotions

There are different ways to receiving emotions. One way is that you observe something from the target/s and this gives you ideas of what he/she is feeling. Another is that you don't see or hear anything from the target but you just know the emotions involved or you feel the emotion yourself.

When you select a target to receive emotions, it's better if you choose someone who you don't know much. If you practice with someone you know a lot, you may tend to rely on your previous experiences with that person to know what he/she may probably be feeling. On the other hand, receiving emotions from a stranger will leave you no choice but to rely on genuine psychic ability.

Calm all emotions first before reaching out to the target. Envision the target in front of you or around you. To lessen confusion, you can create a link that has a one-way flow of energy so you only receive and not send emotions.

Developing the Psychic Senses

Understanding psychic abilities will help you cope better with being an empath. Some associate empathy as a manifestation of an overactive heart or third eye chakra. Later on, you will learn how to work with chakras to control your abilities better.

Working with the chakras involves sensitizing yourself to subtle energies too. This is why developing your clairvoyance is a helpful (although unnecessary) part of managing life as an empath.

To develop your psychic abilities, you need to go into a mild trance so you can receive psychic information more easily. You must break away from your normal state of awareness so you won't confuse your imagination with what you pick up.

You enter a trance by doing the following:

- Relaxing your entire body

- Closing your eyes

- Minimizing sensory inputs (use a blindfold and earplugs, close your eyes, turn off music, go in a floatation tank, etc.)

- Taking deep, meditative breaths

- Releasing troublesome thoughts and emotions

- Keeping your mind as blank as possible

There are certain situations when you enter a trance normally:

- Before going to sleep

- Right after you wake up

- Relaxing

- Praying

- Meditating

- Dreaming

You will know that you have entered a trance when your attention is focused inwardly rather than what goes on around you and your mental chatter is not that loud.

Aside from learning how to enter a trance and recognize when you're in a trance, you must be familiar with how your mind receives psychic information. This is similar to things popping into your mind or you suddenly remembering something. Take note though, that it's easy to mistake psychic info with imagination, expectations, fears, desires, and the like, so you must start gathering info with a blank slate.

Focus on a target or ask a question. Wait for whatever comes into your mind. This can be anything – a memory, a sound, a voice, visuals, symbols, and more. Remember these and try to record them in some form through writing or describing them over a recorder.

When you notice that the stream of information starts to taper off, or if you suspect that you are just making it up already, stop recording. Look back at what you've gathered and try to interpret them. Record your interpretations as well. Afterwards, seek confirmation about whether your hunch is true or not.

Gradually, you will have a grasp of how your psychic abilities work and what certain signals mean. You will also learn how to distinguish false hunches from true ones.

You may already detect subtle energies, but if you want to sharpen this sense, you can practice by turning your focus inward and noticing how your mind portrays something to you. For example, if someone is really angry, notice what you're sensing. Are you seeing the color red in your mind's eye? Are you feeling heat on your skin? If there are a lot of children around, compare what you sense with when you're with elderly people. Soon, you will be able to learn your intuition's representations of the energies it detects.

Learn the different energies by going into areas or immersing yourself in situations where those are present. You may also look at pictures, watch videos, or listen to songs that evoke them. This will make you work with emotions better, too.

The next chapter is all about chakras – energy centers along your body. You will be more ready to work with them when you have gained the ability to sense energy, but you can jump straight into the exercises if you want.

Chapter 5.

Chakra Development for Empaths

I t's possible for an empath to have weakened chakras when they sacrifice too much for other people. Correcting these weakened chakras will help make things better for the empath. Take note that this is just a brief discussion of chakra development, and there are other things that are not included here such as yoga poses, chakra associations, dietary recommendations, and the likes. However, the information given below will be enough for most matters.

Root Chakra

The root chakra nestled at the base of the spine deals with survival, security, and physical existence. A sick root chakra brings fear, insecurity, and a lack of connectedness to earthly life, while a healthy root chakra brings strength, security, and a readiness to face life's challenges.

Physical tasks, especially those involving the legs and feet, help activate this chakra. Activities done in natural environments such as gardening and fishing will also be helpful.

Grounding involves connecting the root chakra with the energy of the earth. Focus on this chakra to regain your composure and stability in the midst of intense emotions. Red, earthy, or black crystals resonate to the root chakra's energies.

Sacral Chakra

The sacral chakra is stationed in the lower abdomen near the internal and external reproductive organs. It is linked to sexuality, creativity, pleasure, and sexual relationships. A disharmonious sacral chakra results to problems with the sex drive, guilt in achieving pleasure, addictions, or unhealthy relationships. When this chakra functions well, it enables fulfilling intimate connections and a balanced attitude towards pleasure.

Indulging in sensual, pleasurable experiences help soothe the sacral chakra. Doing these activities with a loving partner will be more effective in targeting the sacral chakra than being alone.

Because the sacral chakra is orange, orange crystals and gemstones may be used when focusing on this chakra. Focus here to improve your connections with those you are intimate with.

Solar Plexus Chakra

The solar plexus is within the abdomen and it's closely related to the digestive system because it absorbs energy and circulates it all throughout the energetic channels of the subtle body. The person's identity, ego, and will are solar plexus attributes.

Issues with the solar plexus shows up as extremes: powerlessness or dominance, an overinflated ego or lack of self-esteem. When the solar plexus is alright, the person is responsible with how he/she uses his/her own power, and he/she has a healthy self-esteem.

Effortful actions stimulate the solar plexus chakra because this is where a person's energy is centered. Examples of these are vigorous activities, competitive tasks, martial arts, and the likes.

Yellow crystals are best suited for solar plexus work. If you want to regain your sense of self and strengthen your boundaries, meditate on the solar plexus chakra.

Heart Chakra

The heart chakra serves as the energetic counterpart of the physical heart. It is believed to be the center where emotions are generated and felt.

When the heart chakra is blocked, the person may be having difficulties with processing emotions. He/she may also be prone to harboring negative feelings. When it is open, the chakra creates positive emotions and a love for one's self and for other people.

Clearing the heart chakra is done by doing things that evoke positive sentiments towards others, such as helping those in need, being with family and friends, or doing something enjoyable with other people.

Green colored gems are recommended for working with the heart chakra. To release negative emotions and attract positive ones, work on this chakra.

Throat Chakra

The throat chakra is linked to communication, expression, and the intellect. A weak throat chakra may be linked to difficulties in expressing one's self, lying, gossiping, overthinking or not thinking properly. A properly functioning throat chakra bestows good communication skills and clear thought.

Activities that balance the throat chakra are those that involve exercising one's thoughts and expressing them. Singing, reciting stories or poems, and other vocal exercises will also stimulate chakra.

Blue crystals are used for connecting to the throat chakra. Empaths may need to pay attention to this chakra because they tend to suppress their thoughts to prevent stirring up negative emotions around them.

Third Eye Chakra

The third eye chakra is between the two eyes deep within the head. It gives sight – both physical and clairvoyant sight. This chakra pertains to one's psychic abilities, abstract thought, and imagination.

A diseased third eye chakra may trigger mental difficulties, confusion, and inability to use psychic abilities. A strong third eye chakra enhances psychic abilities and strengthens the mind.

Meditation, contemplation, dream work, and mystical practices are some of the activities that can cleanse and empower the third eye chakra.

Indigo-colored or deep blue crystals resonate with the third eye chakra. A hyperactive third eye chakra may cause an empath's abilities to become overwhelming. If this is the case, visualizing one's third eye to slow down a bit may help control the symptoms.

Crown Chakra

The crown chakra is the highest of the major chakras. It symbolizes the unification of one's self to the Divine.

Spirituality, higher consciousness, and divine connection are the areas that pertain to the crown chakra.

Crown chakra imbalances may point to lack of spirituality, excessive materialism, and possibly insanity. When it is balanced, it gives spiritual fulfillment and a feeling of connectedness with the divine.

Spiritual acts such as dedicating one's life to God, sacrificing one's self for greater causes, and fervent praying can help purify the crown chakra.

Purple or white crystals are recommended for handling the crown chakra. Empaths usually have a strong crown chakra. If you think you need help from the spirit world, tap into the energies of this chakra.

Chapter 6 tackles a major challenge of being an empath: managing emotions. Although it is applicable to other people, it will matter to you a lot.

Chapter 6.

Emotional Management for Empaths

Empaths need to manage their emotions since they tend to feel more than the average person. Thankfully, there are a lot of techniques for achieving control over feelings regardless of how strong they seem to be.

Managing Undesirable Emotions

If you dislike how you feel, you can make it subside through the following methods:

Calm Down

Emotions are a form of stimulation because they trigger changes in the body (example: fear causes the heart rate to speed up and increases muscle tension) and mind (emotions bring up thoughts and memories that are relevant to them). Calming down decreases this stimulation and weakens the impact of emotion.

Taking deep, slow, and even breaths is one easy way to calm down. Just as emotions affect how one breathes, deliberately controlling it will also affect what one feels. Notice what you feel and how you breathe. If you want to change your emotion, change your breathing pattern.

Another is to relax tense muscles – this will tell your brain that everything is alright so it will stop releasing hormones that trigger unpleasant sensations. Move around freely to affirm that you are free to do whatever you wish.

Stop entertaining aggravating thoughts and shift to relaxing thoughts. Bring up memories of you being peaceful and comfortable. You can also focus on something that you are looking forward to.

Change Your Perspective

What you feel is affected by how you think about the situation. If you change how you describe what's happening, or if you look at it from a different perspective, you will likewise change how you emotionally respond to it. For example, if someone is really angry, instead of blaming yourself like what empaths usually do, you can think that they're just feeling ill, so they can't help but release their frustration on others.

Focus On Your Priorities

There is simply no end to things that has the potential to bother you. You can do something about a few of them, while the rest are not within your power to control. If you try to control everything that happens to you, you'll just be more frustrated. However, your reaction to the things that happen to you are completely within your control.

What you focus on determines how you feel and think. If something demands your undivided attention, consider whether it's truly worth minding. The more of your energy that you spend for something, the less energy you will have for the things that are important. Because of this, you must decide what's worth focusing on and let go of the rest.

Fake the Emotion

The brain monitors the condition of the different parts of the body and it creates emotional responses based on what it senses. If your body language expresses a particular emotion, your brain will think that you are feeling the emotion, thus it will release hormones that will support it. As an example, grinning for at least three minutes will make a person happy even if he or she isn't really feeling upbeat. Making "power poses" such as standing with a wide stance and arms overhead will make a nervous person feel more self-assured. Pretend that you are already feeling your desired emotion and make your behavior reflect it. Soon enough, you will feel the emotion.

Process It

Thinking about whatever you're feeling will lessen its influence. This is because emotions are designed to be felt and acted upon. Thinking introduces additional factors to the process so it can potentially derail the process. It can also question the assumptions that support the emotions.

Emotions guide a person to do something in particular without having to think about it. If you think about the situation, you tell yourself that you intend to make a conscious choice, so the emotions may wane as it's not that necessary anymore.

Expressing It

Emotions are a form of energy because they are meant to propel the person into action. If you dislike the direction that your emotions are leading you towards, release it through a different way. You can use anger as a force to power you through a tedious chore, or you can turn sadness into a catalyst for touching poetry, for example. You can also write about what you feel or talk about it to someone who is willing to listen. This will help you review it more objectively.

Cultivating Positive Emotions

Being an empath makes one vulnerable to negativities such as:

- Anger

- Resentment

- Disgust

- Anxiety

- Fear

- Grief

- Guilt

- Insecurity

- Feeling Overwhelmed

- Feeling Helpless

- Internal Conflict

Because you are extra-sensitive to emotions, it's healthier if you stop holding on to negative emotions and gravitate more to positive ones. The more often you do this, the more natural it will be to you until it becomes part of your normal, everyday "aura".

Aside from the techniques mentioned about, you can let go of unpleasant emotions through the following methods:

- Leaving the cause or trigger of the emotion

- Visualizing the emotions as fading into nothingness

- Exercising

- Creating affirmations and reciting them regularly

- Doing something enjoyable and fulfilling

- Staying with people who make you happy

- Labeling emotions so you can consider it for what it is instead of just feeling it

- Relabeling the emotion into something more positive (example: fear into excitement, anger into motivation, sadness into cherishing)

- Meditating

- Observing whatever you feel in a detached manner

- Reminding yourself that you are not your emotions and they will soon pass

- Focusing more on things and thoughts that foster positive feelings

- Pretending the emotion is a person and talking to it to know it's message

- Thanking the emotion for its help

- Viewing the emotion in a more positive light

- Reminding yourself of good things about the feeling or thing that is bothering you

- Finding out the purpose of the emotion and doing something about it

Emotions are tools that are meant to help us act on things. Don't let them use you but learn to use them instead. Once you do, not only will you survive being an empath, you will even be someone who can empower other people.

Chapter 7.

A Toolbox of Techniques for the Empath

These are some of the best tools that an empath will most likely need. Although the main challenge of being an empath is learning how to have better emotional management, this chapter deals with more specific issues that are also as important as handling emotions well.

Deal With Indecisiveness

Take time in deciding for as long as the situation allows it. Ask for more time if you really need to think things over, and if you can afford to wait longer. Pretend that you have already decided upon something. This will change your mood, and your perspective will follow. This will allow you to see things more clearly so you can decide more easily.

Reduce the Risk of being Drained

These are situations where it's likely that you will be drained:

- Being obsessed

- Excessively talked to

- Trying to be accepted

- Feeling guilty

- Being a martyr

- Forcing yourself or being forced to act unnaturally

- Interacting with someone who is dishonest or hiding something

- Being taken advantage of

- Having loveless relationships

- Drama

- Being abused

- Someone depending on you too much

- Being controlled

- Feeling unwelcome

- Being insecure

- Feeling unsafe

- Trying hard to fit in/be accepted

- Experiencing Chronic Fatigue or other illnesses

Pay attention to situations when you feel uncomfortable or depleted. Whenever you encounter these again, ask yourself if you really need to go through it. If yes, defend yourself using the techniques you've learned in this book. If no, forget about it or pass it on to another person.

Set Limits and Boundaries

You must have a firm idea of who you are, what your priorities are, what your goals are and what you want to do. Using these ideas, set boundaries and do not let people push them.

Always remember that there are times when people do not really need you but they will just take advantage of your caring nature. Some may even enjoy seeing you do so much without asking for anything in return. Take care of yourself first and foremost. You are responsible for your own wellbeing.

Only help when it's really needed and when doing so will not harm you. If you notice that a person has become dependent on you, be kind by letting him/her stand on his/her own feet. It may feel good to be needed but you are just making both of you weak.

Stop Being a Martyr

Stop feeling guilty about things that you don't really need to feel guilty for. Guilt is an energy drain. Believe that whatever you did or did not do has some beneficial effect to others and to yourself.

Cease worrying too much about other people. Although you know you can help them, if they don't ask for help, it's likely that they don't need help at all. There are things that they have to resolve for themselves for their own personal growth.

Ask yourself, are you concerned about others because you want to feel needed and important? Is it also possible that you want to control the other person but you don't want to appear mean, so you disguise it as helping? Being honest with yourself will free you from patterns of unhealthy behaviors.

Develop a Strong Identity

Empathizing so much with other people can make your identity changeable. This may result from wanting to please other people or to make them feel they are not alone. This may earn you some friends for the short term, but they will eventually mistrust you when they notice that you keep on changing depending on who you're with.

Keep in mind that people will be fine without you modifying yourself to please them. They will appreciate a person who is consistent rather than someone who fakes things to gain approval. Also, if they want you to think and act a certain way, they don't really care about you but they just want to manipulate you. Don't give them that chance – you are just encouraging them to be abusive not only to you but perhaps to others as well.

Build Self Confidence

An empath will be aware when people around them do not have pleasant thoughts and feelings about them. This makes an empath become more prone to developing insecurities than those who are oblivious to others' reactions towards them. Because of this, empaths may develop social anxieties and feel bad about themselves, always blaming themselves for not being accepted in a group.

If you're having problems with your self-esteem, remember that nobody is perfect, and nobody has to be. Learn to accept yourself for who you are despite what others think about you. You don't need to feel bad when they don't know who you really are or don't like you if you know and like yourself. Remember – even if they can affect how you feel, you can change how you feel too. Choose to feel good.

Choose Your Company

Surround yourself with people who support you. Be objective and specify who in your social circles are not that pleasant towards you. Stay away from them even if you feel attached to them. A little distance may make you see them in a more truthful light.

When people want to leave the relationship, don't hold on to them. Those who love and accept you will stay, while those who don't will naturally drift away from you. You don't have to change who you are just to keep them around. Even if very few remain, they are those who are worth your company.

Don't be afraid to disappoint or let go of people. You can get over whatever negative emotions that will be involved, but if you keep appeasing them, you will just prolong your agony. Whatever happens, consider it as something that will contribute to spiritual growth.

Don't Take Too Much Responsibilities

Even if you feel emotionally compelled to help someone or do things, you must protect yourself so you won't stretch yourself thin. This is especially important if you have grown so used to being kind.

As an empath, you may be compelled to help others more than necessary because you feel their negative emotions. However, always remember that you are not them, and it's possible that you are stopping them from maturing because you do things that they are supposed to do themselves. Sometimes, you also have to let them face the consequences of their actions or deal with unpleasant emotions so they will become stronger people.

People may resent you for not helping them as you usually do, but in the end, your feelings are yours and their feelings are theirs. If you want to help others, set limits as to how and when you will do this. Don't let it interfere with how you want to live your life. After all, it's your life, not theirs.

Express Yourself

Empaths are so used to absorbing emotions of those around them that they also tend to keep in what they really feel. They do not want to bother others because that will bother them too! However, once you learn how to separate your own self from other people, you will take care of yourself better. One of the first steps of doing that is to know what's really in your heart and say it openly. Not everyone is an empath like you. You need to spell it out for them.

Remember: everyone and everything is connected, and you as an empath can feel this connection more than anyone else. However, you are still you so your prime responsibility is yourself. Help when you can, but be merciful to yourself. We can only give what we have. Nourish yourself so you will have plenty to share.

Conclusion

Being an empath means being capable of sensing and giving more than the ordinary person. Whatever you decide to do with your gift is ultimately your decision, but may it be something that will help you grow as an individual. Not everyone is like you and not everyone can do what you can. Because of this, try to use your gifts in ways that will benefit humanity, or at least those who are close to you.

Most importantly, never lose sight of yourself despite having a wider perspective than normal. Although you may feel others more strongly, what's inside you matters, too. Once you've taken care of yourself, you will be more capable of serving others. Let them help you, too – being kind feels nice.

We are all linked to each other whether this is felt or not. As one who feels this deeply, you have the most potential to benefit from this connection. May this fill you with joy and courage.

Lastly, if you enjoyed reading the book, could you please take time to share your views with us by posting a review on Amazon? Having a positive review from you helps the book stay on top of the ranks, so we can continue to reach those who can benefit from the information shared within the book. It'd be highly appreciated!

To your success.

Book #3

Persuasion

The Definitive Guide to

Understanding Influence, Mindcontrol and NLP

INTRODUCTION

Congratulations on purchasing this book, and thank you for doing so.

This book is about the power you hold within you, and how to use that power to get what you want out of your life. The art of persuasion can aid you in reaching any goal, of changing the minds of both yourself, and others, and can be the beginning of any positive change. You are in charge, and you already hold the keys to success. You just need to understand what those keys and skills are, and how to use them.

The following book, and the chapters contained within, will discuss and introduce you to the fine arts of persuasion, understanding, influence, mind control, and NLP (or Neuro Linguistic Programming). This book will explain how to use and utilize these tools in everyday application to your advantage, and how to become better at using these skills to attain any goal you hope to. You will learn what these skills are, how they work, the benefits of possessing these skill sets, and how to improve your abilities. Practical applications for use of these skills is possible, and with knowledge, comes power. With power, comes achieving your goals and getting what you want out of your life.

There are a vast array of books and literature on the subjects we will go over in this book on the market today, thank you again for choosing this one! Every effort was made to ensure this book is full of as much useful information and practical applications as possible, please enjoy!

CHAPTER 1

The Art of Persuasion

Persuasion is a powerful tool. If you can persuade another person that you are right, anything is possible. But first, let's start with the basics. What is persuasion? Persuasion, or the act of persuading, is the ability to change another's way of thinking by convincing the other individual that your belief, which is grounded on assurance, is correct. Assurance can be making a declaration and not just a statement. Being confident in your words, thoughts, and ideas exudes self-confidence. People are more apt to listen to someone who makes assertions in a confident manner. But, to have the self-assurance needed to persuade another person, knowledge is required. You must know what you are speaking about with authority for others to concede to your ideas or wants. Whatever the end-goal is, you need to know a lot about it. Do your homework and be ready to explain why you are correct. It is important to note, that authority does not equal pushy. In fact, being too pushy or in-your-face with someone is a huge turn-off, and will often be met with immediate rejection of your idea or desire.

There are many ways to persuade another person that your way of thinking is right, and there also many degrees of persuasion one can use, from a subtle suggestion, to outright pressure. Swaying someone to think like you do, to see things your way, is useful and doesn't necessarily mean they need to be coerced. Sometimes, people want to be one the same page as you, they just need a little help getting there!

So, how do you convince another person that they should agree with you, or do what you want, for both their benefit and your own?

The first step is understanding that to persuade an individual, they should be open to listening to you. Someone that has no desire to hear you out will not be open to the conversation necessary to understand where you are coming from, and why you feel or think as you do. Your target audience is someone that is willing to hear you out, think about what you are saying, and be open to your suggestion. Knowing who you are trying to persuade is key. To reach your audience, whether it's your significant other or a room full of peers, you should know others inside and out, front to back. If you are interacting with someone who is passive and meek, tone down your voice and use less aggressive language. If you want to convince your very outgoing friend that your plan is more desirable than theirs, turn up the vocal volume and get amped when you speak about what you want. In fact, it is important to keep in mind that who you are trying to persuade is another human, just like you, and not a target or opponent. People want and crave connection. Being persuasive isn't about winning someone else over, or beating them, it is about convincing them that you only want what is best for them and yourself. Individuals you have regular conversations with, or people that you have already formed a relationship with are easier to persuade and more open to your ideas as there is already a relationship base in place. These are people that you engage and connect with about any number of things. You understand what is important to them, how they prioritize their lives, and what makes them tick. Using what you know about another person is vital.

Other small tactics that are useful when trying to be persuasive are subtle compliments. Being genuine in your compliment is the goal, overt flattery makes others feel like you are fake. And being fake will not get you far. Rather than complementing someone for their appearance or a materialistic nicety, compliment them on their brain. Saying things like, "You know a lot about the topic", rather than "Oh, I love your hairstyle", make for more meaningful and respectful interactions. Utilizing positive words, rather than negative language also help set the tone for the conversation. Saying words like "empathize, understand," and using phrases like, "I agree, however", or "I appreciate your opinion, but", are non-aggressive yet firm ways to let the other party know that while you may not agree with their idea or opinion, you understand their thought process and appreciate their opinions.

Now that we understand the basics of persuading someone you know, what about persuading someone who you have never met before? You obviously won't know this person on a deeper level, and knowing their motivations at first sight isn't an option, so how do we get those we don't know on our side?

People tend to lean their opinions or beliefs systems towards people they like. The easiest way to get someone to like you, is for them to feel like YOU like THEM. Engage with someone you don't know with your whole being, turn physically toward them, smile, and express interest in them and what they have to say. Use your nonverbal body queues to express your interest in them. Introduce yourself, and be open to being vulnerable. The more another person knows about you, the more they are willing to divulge about themselves. When they are speaking, don't just hear them. Listen. Listening as a means to reply is felt, and somehow, people always no when you aren't listening to their words, but merely waiting for your chance to respond. If you make the interaction all about you, you will be met with rejection almost immediately. Show your interest and excitement about meeting someone new, allow them the floor as much as possible, and wait. The more you listen, the more they talk. The more they talk, the more you learn. And, the more you learn about someone, the more you understand them.

Another tactic to persuade another person to agree with you is touch. Not aggressive hand-holding, or high-fives, but often a simple touch of your finger on their upper arm in a quick and nondescript manner creates a huge physiological response in the human body. Chemicals are released in the brain, signaling a sign of embrace, acceptance, and often is barely registered. Timing is key when reaching out to someone who is almost virtually unknown to you. If you choose to try this technique of persuasion, the execution needs to be after the initial greeting has given way to positive feedback and conversation. Making sure to be looking the other person in the face, and being swift and confident in your gesture makes it feel more natural, and not an invasion of personal space. It gives a sense of welcoming, the budding of understanding and even friendship.

When considering persuasion, it is always best to remember that practice and practical application only makes you more persuasive.

CHAPTER 2

Understanding, And How
to Use It

To get what you want from other's, you need to be able to understand them. Now, this is easy when dealing with family, friends, coworkers, and people you have daily or regular contact with. You talk about a myriad of things, know what they think and feel, and why they feel as they do. And if you don't understand them, it isn't hard to ask. Relationships that have already been established make for easier understanding, you "get them" and where they are coming from, so persuading someone you know is not always that hard of a feat. New acquaintances, people you have never encountered before, whether you are trying to sale them something, or give a talk, now that is much more difficult. With no base to go on, how does one convince another to agree? Well, the most important detail is figuring out who your target audience is, what you think they may feel, and make initial contact all about them.

Humans are a self-absorbed species. We spend most of our time thinking about our lives. What do we want, how do we get it, who do we love and care for, how's our financial health, are we feeling okay physically? It goes without saying that most of us are consistently absorbed with thoughts of our own lives and we are driven based on our own circumstances. So, how do we get to know someone quickly so that we may create the relationship base needed to be able to persuade them?

We talk about them, with them!

Whether speaking before an audience, or trying to sell a product to the public, the easiest way to get to know someone is to get them talking about themselves. Asking open ended questions that can't end with a yes or no answer, listening to them, vesting your time and total attention to them, and engaging allows others to open up about themselves. The more we know about another person, the more we understand who they are, what they believe, and how we can go about persuading them to agree with us. We need to be able to understand their motivations, and appeal to those things specifically.

An effective way to get another to talk about themselves is to ask a question, and wait. After the individual answers the question you posed to them, do not reply immediately. Pause, making eye contact, and wait a second or two before speaking or responding back. Humans often feel compelled to fill empty silences, and many times when we wait a moment before replying or asking a follow up question, an individual will continue speaking to fill the space. Try it out! This tactic does not always work, and can make for an awkward silence, so timing silence is key. Wait too long, and both you and the other party will feel a little out of place, but waiting just a beat or two often compels the other person to fill the silence. This gives you even more knowledge than you asked for, and can only benefit you and your goals.

Since it is mentioned in the last paragraph, let's go over timing and its importance when considering persuasion.

Timing is of the utmost importance, and not just during a conversation. When trying to appeal to an individual or audience, the timing of persuasion and the reason for it is key. If you want to sell something, steer the conversation towards the future. What one does not have now, they may soon need and be left wanting. It is better to buy now, and save the risk of not having what they need when they need it. If arguing a case, or debating about why your opinion is correct, steer the conversation to the past. Using examples of previous let downs or negative outcomes, and why your opinion or idea will prevent the past from repeating itself is a very compelling idea. Nobody wants to feel negative emotions like foolishness, stupidity, or ignorance. A good way to get others to open to your way of thought is by the simple but effective reminder that repeating mistakes of the past is unavoidable, unless a change is made. And you can offer that change by way of your ideas, thoughts, or actions. If giving a presentation, utilize the present state of things. Going over what is happening now and what the current issues are is a good and effective lead in to discuss what has happened in the past, and what may happen in the future. Using the present, past, and future examples as a base for your ideas makes for a compelling and effective argument.

Remember, that while timing is key, it is hard for someone to argue logic. Know your facts, know your goals, and know how you want to get there. Appealing to one's sense of logic appeals to one's sense of intelligence. People want to feel like they are making a smart decision, and you can offer them that. There are other individuals who base their choices on emotion. Once you understand what makes them feel, you can use it to your advantage to convince them that you know exactly how they feel, and you can help them. Another final aspect to consider is your authority on what you want people to agree with. Your authority can be your expertise, your experiences, or even just the way you carry yourself and appear. Be confident, know what you want, and learn to understand how to get others to agree with you by understanding the way they think. If it is important to them, it is important to you. You are now already on the same page about one thing, and a base is now created to build the trust needed for them to empathize and agree with what you think.

CHAPTER 3

Using Influence

Influence is a powerful, but often subtle tool. The ability to affect or change someone's opinion, or create a change in circumstances without forcing the change directly is an art form all its own. Creating changes or conditions as situations develop creates lasting impact. It can make others sit up and take notice of you and your presence, and often create a perception of you that may make others want to defer to you in the future. In this chapter, we will go over how to create influence, how to build your skills in regards to influencing others, and how to utilize the influence you have built to achieve your goals.

Influence is based on basic, but key factors. Let's start with a room full of people whom you do not know. Your entrance into this room is vital. You may not know anyone, but not everyone present will know this. Presenting yourself in the most flattering way within the first few seconds will often dictate the way everyone in the room sees you. Smile as you enter the room, walking with your back and head in straight but relaxed alignment. Taking time not to rush or enter too slowly, imagine you are just walking into a room in your home. An often-effective trick to make you seem more approachable is to give a short wave, as if you are acknowledging someone you know. This makes others assume that someone else in the room already knows you, and that in and of itself makes you seem more likeable or interesting.

When first meeting someone, making eye contact and firmly shaking their hand while smiling boosts your effective charisma with the other individual. Charisma is more about how you make the other person feel when they are in your presence. Charisma is not necessarily about being the life of the party. To work on your charisma, first consider your own strengths. Are you humorous? Are you already outgoing and friendly? Do you tend to be shy and quieter? You can use any of your strengths to your advantage, it is all about understanding how to use them. If you are more of an introvert, pick one or two people off to the side of the crowd or room to engage with. When initiating communication, use your quieter presence to let others do more of the talking, and only steer the conversation in the direction you want it to go into when necessary. As we have established previously, people love to talk about themselves! If you are outgoing, place yourself in a position of power, feel free to approach larger groupings of people and greet them. Again, use your strengths to your advantage.

People that hold sway over others can attest, influence is all about give and take. When people feel, a relationship is based on reciprocation, they trust the relationship easier and sooner, and have less reservations. Try asking a small favor of someone, and then in turn offering them the same in return. An example would be offering to hold someone's place in line while they use the restroom, taking notes for them while they excuse themselves momentarily during a meeting or presentation, and then asking them to do the same for you upon their return. This give and take lays a foundation of comradery, like you and the other party are already friendly. And people that feel like you like them, like you in return.

Building relationships overnight is not easy, but it can be easier by being friendly. Smiling and eye contact play a role in how you make other people feel. If you project that you are happy to see others, that you are happy to be speaking with them, they will in turn feel happy to be communicating with you. Your body language speaks volumes, and others pick up on what you are conveying with yours, even if they aren't fully aware of it. When engaging with another, take note in how they are standing or sitting. If they are standing with their arms at their sides, you should mimic their stance. Mimicking someone's body language is another way of building an unspoken but solid foundation. If they are clearly exhibiting stress, mimic their stance. An example of this would be if their arms are crossed over the front of their body in defensive pose. After a few minutes of conversation, move your arms to a more relaxed and natural position. In most instances, the person you are communicating with will subconsciously reposition their body language to mimic your own. This is an example of how you are already gaining influence and trust with someone who you barely know.

When talking to individuals you want to gain influence over, another aspect to consider is your own attitude towards them. We know that our physical body language plays a role, and that reciprocating is important as well, but just as important is how you project yourself. Greeting another with a smile is great, but now that the conversation has started, maintain a neutral but relaxed facial expression. Staying involved and being attentive when others speak again makes them feel good speaking with you. Asking questions per the flow of conversation shows that you are listening to them, and everyone wants to be heard. Being respectful, calm, and diplomatic in your interactions makes you more friendly and approachable. Showing gratitude for their time, and being appreciated will encourage others to appreciate your attention and time in return.

A good way to connect with others is to be authentic in your communications with them. You want to convey that you are sincere, that you are invested in what is important to them. Finding common ground and things that you can easily agree on leads to topics that they are more emotionally connected to. Be emotionally curious by asking questions that will elicit an emotional opinion or feeling from the other party. This helps you understand what is important to them, and therefore how to exert your influence with them on not just by using a logical stance, but by an emotional appeal.

A final consideration to help you influence others is people's desire to belong. People want to feel like they are part of a group or movement, that they are included and belong with their peers. When you express authority on a topic or opinion or desire, support your stance with evidence. Statements that include others who agree with you, or statistical facts that indicate trends within the topic, make others pause and consider who else agrees with you, why your opinion is accurate or right, and why they too should align their opinions with your own.

Once you have established a base relationship with another person, whether it be simple and basic, or deep and complex, influencing them is not that difficult. If you are met with resistance, ask more questions. Many times, people resist an idea or a change for many reasons than those that rest on the surface. Express a desire to know why they do not agree, empathize with their reasons for resistance, and listen to why they hesitate. Often, once you understand why they reject your influence, you can redirect or discuss other viable reasons for them to change their viewpoint for your benefit, and theirs too.

CHAPTER 4

Mind Control

Mind control sounds like a devious plot in a movie, but you have most likely experienced it many times a day for many years and never noticed it. Mind control, or the idea of thought-reform, is a controversial theory and practice, but one that does not necessarily mean tricking and scheming. As a matter of fact, mind control can be as simple as subliminal suggestion used to steer one in the direction you want rather than the direction they were going autonomously.

There are many schools of thought in regards to mind control, but for this book, let's look at a common example of mind control to start. Color, smell, sight, sound, and taste are used on the consumer by every company selling a product to advance their customers and sales. When you enter your local grocery store, often there are fresh cut flowers at the entrance. Now, how often have you bought those flowers? Chances are, never, if maybe a time or two because you forgot a special occasion. Grocers use the presence of these flowers as a means of manipulating the subconscious of their customers. Fresh cut flowers are, well, fresh. Ripe. Pleasant. They subliminally convey they thought of freshness, and your local grocery store wants you to be thinking about all the fresh produce they have waiting for you. More often, these grocers make more on the sale of their fresh produce over name brand canned and frozen produce, and if you buy the produce they have available, more of your dollars go in their pocket as opposed to mass production companies.

Every day, you are exposed to one form of mind control or another. Product placement on television and in movies. The music you hear in a store or even an elevator. Friends that are so convincing, you can't help but agree, or you find yourself always saying yes to them. In this chapter, we will go over some techniques of mind control, also known as coercive persuasion, and how you can achieve goals by using these techniques to your advantage.

Re-education is a very optimal, but controversial tool in mind control. The ability to re-educate another person's previous thought process or beliefs is possible, but can take time. At the heart of re-education sits repetition. I repeat, repetition. By repeating the same belief, idea, or thought to another person, repeatedly, you are impressing upon them the change from their own ideas towards your own. And this repetition leads to immersion in the idea or action you want them to follow. Being immersed in an idea, the idea in question always being repeated, the idea or goal always being spoken of, leads to the individual re-examining their previous feelings about the issue. Re-examining one's feelings often leads to them coming to a new conclusion. Your conclusion. You have just exerted a form of mind control on another individual, and now they agree with you.

Priming an individual is another effective way to get what you want. Some who see this activity negatively may refer to in as indoctrination, but the goal is not to necessarily start a cult. You are just trying to get others to agree with you, and are trying to use all the available tools you possess to your advantage. Priming involves softening a person towards you and your ideas, easing them into the thought that you know what is best. Softening can include hours of conversation, empathizing with them and showing them that you care or love them. You care about what happens, you understand them. Once you have a foundation of trust through understanding and priming, soft persuasion towards the new idea, belief, or action can be introduced. It is imperative that you have formed a mutual bond or respect with the person who you want to influence. And it is a given that change takes time.

A few techniques to help you on your path to persuasion using coercion may involve thinking for others, being specific in your logic and requests, creating a real sense of urgency, and stressing the importance of your goal or idea. When presenting someone with a change in long held ideas or requests, thinking for them takes the pressure of deciding off them. People often have enough on their mental plates as it is, you shouldn't be asking them to take on more, especially when you can do the heavy lifting for them. Explain exactly why they should see things your way, offering as many examples as possible as to the correctness to your idea, proof that what you want is not only right, but it is proven to be effective or accurate. Once you have specifically lined out why they should agree with you, tell them what is next and why things need to be done your way. Be friendly but as firm and confident in your pitch to them as you need be, and often discouraging questions until you are finished explaining your stance helps steer others in your direction. They often forget their questions or objections as they listen to you explain what you want, why, and what you think needs to happen next to achieve the goal. It is all about the goal.

While we are on the subject of your goals and what you want to achieve, it is imperative to stress the importance of what you want to achieve. If others are consistently being spoken with on how important the idea or goal is, and specifics on why it is so important, eventually they start to see your idea as more than just something you want, but an issue of utmost importance. Your thought or goal becomes something more, and it should be more to you too. it should be a movement. A goal doesn't have to be a social ideal to be a movement, you just need others to feel it's importance as much as you do. Everyone wants to be on the right side of history, no matter how big or small the issue is. And all it takes is someone to see your want as a matter that needs to be addressed or adjusted, and where there is one person who agrees with you, there are two, and more soon to follow.

So, your idea, goal, or thought is now more than just something you want. Other people want it too. And it is not just important, it is imperative. And it needs to happen now. Creating a sense of urgency is another effective form of utilizing mind control techniques to your benefit. Making urgent statements, or claiming that this situation is time sensitive will create an emotional response in those you wish to influence or persuade. A specific deadline needs to be in place, but the idea that this can't wait long needs to be an underlying sentiment. The quicker you get other people on board, the more important you convince them your want is, the more urgent they believe things are, the less resistance you will run into. As it was mentioned previously, repeating equals results. The more information backing your idea or goal people are given, the more likely they will let you think for them and just go with the flow. The more urgent the matter is, the less time people have to ask discouraging questions or second guess their shift in ideas.

Being consistent is the most important aspect of implementing mind control techniques to get what you want. Consistently repeating what you want, and be consistent when rejecting old ideas or goals. Be consistent when speaking about what needs to happen, when and why. These factors should be underlined, in bold print, repeated regularly, and the time sensitivity need to be stressed.

There is nothing wrong with being a little pushy to get what you want out of your life. Another great technique when using mind control is to ask small things of others, or asking for small changes in another's ideas, and then expanding from there. Let's use a raise from your employer as an example. If you want a decent increase in pay, don't ask for your top dollar pay increase. Ask for a small increase in pay based on your performance and loyalty. Your boss will agree (considering you are worthy of the raise to begin with) and think that they got off cheap keeping you happy. After you have reached the first step in reaching your ultimate pay goal, ask for more work. Let your employer know you are more than happy taking on more responsibility. You can possibly save them money if you are doing more work than before, they may not have to hire another employee to work weekends if you are willing to come in for a few hours on a Saturday.

Now, you have a pay increase, but you have more responsibility. It only seems fair that you are paid a little more now that you are a more valuable resource for your employer to utilize. It's better they give you another slight pay increase to cover your knowledge and expertise in the workplace than bother trying to hire another employee to replace you. You see how simple it can be? Now, that isn't saying that you have a boss or employer this would work on, but if you are implementing the other tools you have in your fast-growing arsenal, you are now a very well-liked employee and co-worker who knows how to influence and persuade others to see things the way you do. Your employer may not like the idea of paying you even more than before, but sometimes it's not just your work ethic that matters, sometimes it's what you bring to the table for everyone you encounter.

It is not easy to say no to someone who you feel a debt to. The final technique of mood control we should consider is generosity. You should always strive to give more than you take from others. When you give more of your time, your effort, your attention, to others, they appreciate it. They remember it. And, when the time comes that you want something in return, it is much harder to say no, or disagree, or refuse to cooperate with another who has freely offered up so much to them. Even in circumstances or changes others may not want to agree or get on board with, if they know that you have been offered the same courtesy by you previously, they find it hard to go against you. It falls back to persuasion, influence, and reciprocation. Most often, those that you have committed your time and attention to will return the favor. Even if you are met with resistance by someone who you have given to, a gentle reminder of what you have done for them is often all that is needed to get them on board with what you want. Sometimes it isn't the loudest voice in the room that matters, but the most consistent and softest from the individual who has done the most to help others. That soft but firm voice can be yours, you only need to take your opportunities as they present themselves.

CHAPTER 5

NLP (Neuro-Linguistic Programming)

We have delved into the art of persuasion, what it is, and how to start practicing your ability to persuading others. We have discussed how to understand others, and how understanding others can benefit you in your goals. We know that gaining and using influence to achieve our desires is possible. We have even discussed mind-control and many of its methods, and how to put these methods to everyday use. Now, we are digging deeper, into the world of Neuro-Linguistic Programming, or NLP for short.

NLP was founded and introduced by Richard Brandler and John Grinder in Santa Cruz, California in the 1970's amidst the Human Potential Movement. The Human Potential Movement was a psychotherapeutic movement that took a humanistic approach to people and their woes. The focus during this movement was personal psychological growth and understanding through many techniques. The most emphasized of these techniques were the use, application, and participation of encounter groups, sensitivity training, and primal therapy.

Encounter groups were a new way of thinking in the therapy world. Individuals participating in this type of therapy met as a group with a trainer to help guide their individual and collective process. Group sessions could last for hours, even days, and the length of the sessions was said to help members become uninhibited, literally exhausting its participants, allowing for an increase of self-awareness through verbal interactions that were not directed or influenced greatly by the trainer. Open displays of all range of emotions were welcomed and encouraged, even displays of rage, hostility, and grief.

Sensitivity training was encouraged to help people become more aware of their own prejudices, their own judgements and assumptions, and to become more sensitive and aware of others and their diversities within their group or workplace. Unstructured discussions amongst the group were encouraged to help increase empathy and embrace differences. This type of training is still popular and is often used within business and corporate models to increase harmony among employees and management.

Primal therapy was introduced by Dr. Arthur Janov. Dr. Janov believed that an individual's mental and physical ailments were a manifestation of repressed traumas, usually occurring in childhood. This type of treatment would begin with a patient seeing the therapist on-on-one for three weeks, concluding after fifteen sessions, to explore and get to the root of past traumas and how to overcome them. After the initial one-on-one sessions were completed, the individual patient was introduced to group therapy sessions once to twice a week, with no conclusion or time frame for completion. The focus on these group sessions was to allow patients a safe environment to lose control of their feelings and emotions to process their pain with assistance in a controlled environment, therefore alleviating the effect the trauma's they experienced and the effect those traumatic events had on their overall mental and physical health and well-being.

Now that you have a background on the Human Potential Movement of the 1970's, you will be able to better appreciate the theories behind the introduction of NLP into the world of psychotherapy. The ideas behind NLP are interesting to say the least, and it is important to note that many have discredited the applications and effectiveness of NLP because of what is claimed to be a lack of hard data to support the theories, and the belief that most of the theories of NLP are based on hypothesis only, that is, educated guesses or assumptions made by Bandler and Grinder during their research. Despite the naysayers, NLP is still used as a tool by many self-help personalities, corporations, educators, and psychotherapists today, as well as coaches and for business and management training groups.

The psychotherapeutic applications of NLP are to use the basic principles as a tool to successfully achieve success during instances of persuasion, in negotiations (either in business or personal matters), and during public speaking. For an individual to master the art of NLP, much practice and training will be required to achieve positive results, as NLP demands much control and subtlety. In fact, there are quite a few online workshops and certificate programs available, as well as physical schools dedicated to educating, instructing, and helping those interested in learning how to master the art of NLP. The theories behind NLP are very complex, and can be very hard for the layperson, or someone not familiar with the science and physiology behind the concepts of NLP to understand. In this book, we will introduce the principles and beliefs of what NLSP at is most basic concepts teaches, and how best a person being introduced to the concepts may begin to apply those concepts to achieve their desired goals.

Neuro-Linguistic Programming uses the premise that there is a connection between the language we speak, and the behavior patterns we all exhibit, and that both the way we speak, what words we use, and the way we normally behave can be altered or changed by other's who use NLP to achieve their own goals. That is, that a practitioner of NLP can change or alter another person's normal behaviors or thought patterns. Per the practitioners of NLP, our behavior is best understood based on our five senses, and that our perceptions of reality are subjective and different to everyone based on which of our senses is most prominent at the time of engagement, and that each person's ruling sensory interpretation changes regularly.

In easier terms, NLP states that linguistics (or language) is more than just words we speak, but also how our individual brains process and interpret these communications. Individual processing of this information is stressed, as another vital aspect of NLP is that no two people process and interpret information in the same way. Again, it is important to note that all five senses play a factor in our perception of our lives. So, in theory, by using the practices underlined in NLP, an individual's perception of their reality, their lives, can be altered for the better. Here it should be mentioned that not all people research and study NLP for the sole purpose of practicing NLP techniques on others, but also on themselves to better their life circumstances, or to change things they perceive to be negative in their lives.

To begin the practice of NLP on another person, the most valuable and important aspect is to begin to build a rapport with the other party, or to already have built rapport with the person in question. Rapport is a close relationship that includes mutual understanding of one another's feelings, and an ability to communicate well between yourself and the other party. Rapport is something that you have already built with a close friend or acquaintance, or a family member. When considering the requirements and steps that are needed to begin trying to practice the concepts of NLP on another person, other than already having a close relationship with said individual in question, your influence and the esteem or authority with which the other party views you are significant factors. It is much less difficult to build rapport with someone who looks up to you, sees you as a figure or authority, or defers to you and your knowledge.

So now that you have built rapport with another person, what's next?

The notion is to now begin layering very subtle meaning into your spoken or written interactions with the other person, to begin to implant suggestions in a very light and subconscious way. By stressing key words or phrases when communicating, you are highlighting these key words, and the other person's brain is subconsciously recognizing or remembering them without them being fully aware of what is occurring within their own body. Again, it is important to stress that subtlety is key. Another way to achieve the layered meanings you want to achieve is to use metaphors that can be interpreted in different ways, and the use of double-entendres. An example of a double-entendre was a very ironic and humorous quote by the late Hollywood actress Mae West. Mae once stated "Marriage is a fine institution, but I'm not ready for an institution.". What Mae was getting at is that while the institution of marriage is good and well for others that chose to get married, it also could make those that did marry crazy enough to be institutionalized. It is funny, a play on words, and has a clear double meaning and is open for interpretation.

Emotional speaking, or talking about things that will illicit an emotional response within the other person is also very useful. Knowing what words, phrases, stories, or double-entendres will illicit an emotional response will depend upon how well you know the individual or group of person's you are speaking to. If you understand the other's motivation or the reason being why they want to listen to you. Speak to what you think will create emotion within them. What emotion do you want them to feel? What words make you feel the way you want them to feel? What words make you feel happy? Joy, fun, pleasure, satisfaction, glee, bliss, ecstasy, all are words that convey and illicit happiness. A great example of stimulating a specific emotion, the emotions of optimism and change were invoked in millions of American's during Barack Obama's presidential campaign. The simple phrase, "Yes We Can", along with the simplistic imagery used causes a nationwide emotional response. Simple, to the point, and very effective. When speaking to other's emotions, simple and short is the most effective way to create a specific response in others. The shorter a message is, the more likely the other party's brain will retain it. Our brains can only contain so much information at a time, and it is best to not overload another person with long winded speeches or dialogues. Make an impact. Stress a sentence or phrase that you know will produce the emotional response you hope it does, and then emphasize it by using similar words throughout the communication.

Now that you have built rapport with someone, and you are actively using subtle layering techniques, and speaking to the person's emotions, it is time to become very observant. Watch the tiny non-verbal cues the other party exhibits during this interaction to modify the way you speak to them. Are they moving their eyes away from you, looking at you directly, rolling their eyes to the side? Is there any indication that you need to rephrase a sentence, or use alternative word choices based on how they react? Are their pupils dilating or constricting? Pupillary response is physiological and not a voluntary reaction that is controllable. Pupil dilation as it relates to emotional reaction may indicate sexual arousal, curiosity, or cognitive workload (as in, you are making them think). Pupil constriction can be a sign of a negative response, like fight-or-flight responses are being demonstrated in the body and it is time for you to re-direct the conversation, or disengage altogether and attempt your communication goals later. The faster a pupillary reaction occurs, the stronger their emotional response to the interaction is. Being able to notice pupillary response is something that is easy to practice on a day to day basis, but difficult to master.

Other non-verbal cues that need to be considered are flushing of the skin, their body language, and whether you feel they are being honest with their exchanges, or if there is any indication that they are falsifying certain details, giving false responses, or outright lying. Lying is hard work for the brain, so people who are not telling the truth must work harder at communicating as opposed to people that are being honest and open. People that are lying tend to leave small details out of their stories or responses, as it is easy to forget what specifics were given while lying. If someone mentions a concert they recently attended, but they leave out details or cannot recall what the opening set was, chances are, they aren't being honest. Memory, or the lack of one is another tale. Those that embellish or lie often claim to have a lacking memory, as it is harder to get caught up in a lie if you "can't remember" the information being asked. Correcting what is said is another easy way to tell if someone is not being honest, especially if the individual corrects themselves repeatedly during the interaction. Contradicting information or statements is also a dead giveaway, as is being fidgety, seeming to be nervous or preoccupied, or tense. Just like watching pupil reaction and other non-verbal cues, it is all about keen observation of the overall physical response the other person is exhibiting. Observing other people on this level in an imperceptible way takes a lot of time and practice to master, but with time, your brain can quickly take note of another person's emotional reactions and non-verbal tales. This is important, because it enables you to be able to change their response or way of thinking by interpreting what they are thinking, how you are making them feel, and deciding how to best change their response or thinking to match your own.

The next step in implementing NLP strategies after you have carefully and strategically observed the other person or people, is to then begin to mimic them. By imitating the other persons, you are attempting to create subconscious affiliation with them. This affiliation is another way for those individuals to feel a closer connection with you, as you are similar, even if it is a connection that is solely felt by your generation of it. Other important things to consider mirroring are their mannerisms, and their speech patterns. As mentioned previously, NLP is an art form that takes practice, less your efforts be noticed. If you are not subtle with your techniques, and another person realizes that you are taking on their own affects, they will immediately feel as though you are mocking or imitating them, and many see this as a negative and extremely offensive. Remember, the goal is to get them to trust you, to see you as an ally, someone they could easily have a meaningful connection with, not some hack that is fake or false in their interactions.

Once a rapport has been built, and you have observed non-verbal social queues, created an emotional and significant bond by your design through subtle simulation, it is time to put all your efforts to use. Allow and encourage the other person to talk about themselves, and continuing to be engaged. At the same time, you need to allow the other party to see a sense of openness and vulnerability within yourself, in a real and honest way. It has been stated before, and is now being reiterated again, that people sense falseness, and being fake in your interactions and willingness to be open to them in turn will be admonished. So, by engaging another party or group of people with this give and take will allow an opportunity, created by your own hard work and practices, for others to trust you and what you have to say. Gaining that trust is paramount, as it allows you to begin to steer the conversation in the direction you wish it to go. Steering other's thoughts in the direction you desire allows you the opportunity to set up the exchange to your benefit, and ultimately, gives you the upper hand in getting what you want, persuading others that your ideas or goals are the most logical and accurate, and that you want what everyone else wants too. Remember to elicit emotional states and responses in others as you continue to steer the scenario. Anchoring, again, slight nuanced touch to the upper arm in a natural and quick fashion only furthers your goal. And your goal is easier reached when following these practices that the NLP techniques offers you.

CHAPTER 6

Reflect on Yourself

So far, we have delved into the world of persuasion, and how to get what you want out of life by learning how to understand others for your own benefit, using influence to sway people to see things your way, and how to use simple and not-so-simple mind control and NLP techniques to achieve your goals. But what about you? What do you want out of life? Are you satisfied with all aspects of your world, or could you use a little help persuading yourself to make changes?

This chapter is all about you.

Do you understand yourself well? Do you know who you truly are and what makes you happy? Do you need help achieving what you want? Are you completely self-aware? To make any lasting changes to your own life, you need to know everything you can about you. Sometimes, a little insight into your own psyche goes a long way. Often our own subconscious thoughts and desires aren't apparent. Our actions and choices are often influenced by our subconscious. In order to reach the ultimate self-awareness, understanding all we can about ourselves is key. Sometimes we know exactly how we feel, precisely what we want, but that isn't always the case. There are many ways we can help ourselves learn more, or at least gain a deeper understanding about our inner-most wants or yearnings, and how to change what we are unsatisfied with.

Often, we need others to hold the mirror up for us to see things about who we are more clearly. It helps to focus more on what is present, what it is we need to concentrate on to help us achieve betterment, and not trying to accomplish this task while holding the mirror ourselves allows us more room to focus on the big picture. An objective opinion about what makes us tick can be a priceless jewel when reaching for our best self. Psychoanalysis is one way to achieve this objective view into our psyche. Another good tool for self-discovery may be taking career tests, discovering how we learn best (learning style), or taking personality tests and quizzes.

To reach your full potential, you need to know who you are, warts and all, and what makes you tick. What motivates us is just as important as learning what motivates others. Do you value security over adventure? What are you good at? What are your weaknesses? What is the best thing about you? What in your life gives you joy, and what are you unhappy with? Answering these questions is a good start to understanding yourself.

When making choices, do you think about the consequences, are you logical, always weighing cause and effect, or do your base choice on emotion? Considering that we have all probably based decisions on both the logical choice and our emotions, it becomes clear that with each choice we make, something deeper often lies just below. Consider major events in your life, both good and bad, and how they impacted you in the moment. Are these events still impacting your choices today? Self-evaluation can only help you realize your aspirations.

Do you know that you can persuade and influence yourself to change your mind and improve your life? Self-persuasion is not difficult once you make friends with your true identity and nature. Self-evaluation can be hard at times. We don't always have the best attitudes or ideals, and our priorities aren't always the healthiest for bettering life circumstances. But, once you grasp the big picture on who you are, knowing that YOU CAN CHOOSE TO CHANGE anything you want in your own life is an empowering idea. The task can seem daunting if there are many areas you are unsatisfied with, but you can choose how you tackle making changes.

Starting with your biggest motivator helps many reach their goals. Other people need to see results quickly to become motivated, and so they choose to start with small or easier things to focus on. Whichever direction you choose to use as your starting point, moving forward is the most important step. Reminding yourself daily that some changes do not occur overnight will help keep you focused and prevent feeling frustrated, therefore, giving up too quickly. Looking forward to achieving the change you wish is a positive future outlook and will only help to further change and better your attitude and current viewpoint. Beginning to focus not on what is wrong, but what is right or will be corrected moving forward is possible. To focus your energy on your present accomplishment and further achievement, stop negative and backward thoughts. The point of making a change is not to continually think back on what you don't want, but rather redirecting those negative notions by stopping that train of thought, and going back to the future and what it will look like.

Another way to aid yourself in self-persuasion is to use visual reminders of what your end-goal is. Just like the chubby kid that takes photos of healthy and fit people and posts them on the refrigerator to help motivate and remind them what their end goal is (to lose weight and exercise), visual aids can help keep your goal fresh in your mind. Although the example given is more a negative motivator than a positive one, it can work for you in a similar way. If you want to make more money, envision how you would like to get there, and what your life will look like once you achieve that success. Create a vision board for yourself to look at, save pictures of your ideal, and remind yourself that anyone is possible of anything with work, even you. Daydream about your goal, work on imagining how you will feel when you have accomplished what you desire. Surround yourself with like-minded individuals who share the same goals as you, or with people who support you in reaching for what you want. If you are trying to get healthier or fit, find friends or family who are working towards physical betterment as well, or network with people that already possess the physical health you are working towards. You do not have time to entertain negative people or pessimists who do not support you. Remember, the entire point of making a change is to better your life. Anyone who does not wish you well on your journey and support you does not have your best interests at heart.

A useful tool of NLP that you can use on yourself is to begin re-programming negativity to your advantage. The reason this is a good idea, is that often the fear of failure, or a fear of the unknown, stops one from making positive changes because of the negative connotation that one may feel. You stop yourself before you even start, simply because you do not wish to experience an unpleasant emotion or feeling. Unfortunately, growing pains are a real thing, and negative emotions or physical discomfort are often a part of the process towards betterment. So, what is a way that you can use discomfort or negative feelings to your advantage? And how can you re-program your own mind to overcome these feelings, maybe even come to embrace them?

To start, choose the goal you want to achieve. Think about how you want to reach the goal in question, and the steps you will need to take in order to do so. Now, what is your biggest fear associated with this goal? Or, what causes you to worry or stop yourself from taking the leap and going for it? Focus on that undesirable emotion or action, imagine it is happening now. The idea is to physically induce the experience now, not when it occurs in the future. Yes, the idea of making yourself feel negativity sounds unpleasant, and it is. But you need to feel this way now, because you are going to learn how to master this unpleasantness.

Once you feel this fear, or pain, or embarrassment, whatever negative feeling or emotion that is holding you back, you need to begin to imagine that this thing you are avoiding is in front of you. It is not just an internal reaction, but a physical manifestation that has a life of its own. Imagine what it looks like, how it moves. Does it look like something and have a form, or is it like a cloud or other abstract shape? Do you associate a smell or color with this thing in front of you? You need to be very clear on what this thing is, taking your time until you not only experience the emotions that it elicits within you, but you see in your mind exactly what it is and what it looks like. Now you are facing your fear. Kill it. How you kill or defeat it does not matter.

You can will it to disappear or simply go away from you, you can stomp on it, use a sword. This is your fear, your imagination, and you can dispose of what you do not wish any way you see fit. Have fun with sending your negativity away from you, but be clear on how you accomplish this. Just as you have detailed what this fear looks like, so to do you need to be very clear and consistent with how you get rid of it.

You just killed the fear, worry, anxiety, or whatever adverse emotion or feeling was holding you back. It is gone. Dead. How do you feel? Feel your emotions, and your physical body. Focus on how every separate finger and toe feels, how your skin feels, your arms, legs, scan your entire body and relax every muscle. This activity is also referred to as grounding yourself, and creates a calm and relaxed overall feeling. The negative things that hold you back are now away from you, and you feel at peace. While in this state of relaxation and calm, think of a few ways you can deal with this negative emotion or situation if it arises again in day to day life, and how you can overcome or solve this instance as it happens in real time. Once you have settled on how to beat these worries, write it down on paper to cement it in your mind. Imagine defeating it repeatedly, following the process outlined here as often as you need to. Refer to your written resolutions and ways to solve these problems. They become smaller to you. The thing you fear, or what is holding you back, is no longer huge and menacing, but becomes a small and insignificant issue as you continue to re-program your mind and retrain the way you see and deal with adversity.

As you can clearly see, NLP is a very effective concept, and it can not only be used as an advantageous technique that will help you understand and redirect others for your benefit, but a tool with which you can better your own life and circumstance. As with all the topics we have gone over in this book, practice makes perfect. Utilizing this exercise whenever you can will only make you better at it. The better you are at facing and excising your doubts, worries, uncertainties and concerns, the less they impact your choices, decisions, and actions.

CONCLUSION

You can achieve any goal, see all your ambitions come to fruition, and overcome any obstacle that you want to. Understanding people is the key to realizing your goals. Whether you want to persuade another person to agree with your viewpoint, influence and build rapport with colleagues, or change the way someone sees a topic through the powers of suggestion using mind control techniques, you now have a basic understanding of how to achieve success using the skills and tools outlined in this book. Persuasion and influence are powerful tools that every successful person possesses, and you can be one of those people. You are the captain of your ship, and you can determine not only where you go, but also how you get there, and who takes the journey with you.

The next step to seeing your ambitions realized is to practice what you know. No successful person became the best version of themselves overnight. It takes time, preparation, and repetition to master your skills. Making your new abilities a habit is possible. Give yourself time to put into practice what you now know. No large goal is ever easy to attain, but all goals are achievable if you decide that not only is this what you want, but that you will prevail. You oversee your own life. You are the one who dictates your success, and you can persuade and influence others that not only are you right, but that they are right as well, because they see that you want what is best for everyone. You just have only to make up your mind, and go for it!

Remember that the art of NLP, persuasion, influence and understanding are not only used for the sole purpose of changing others opinions or minds, but your own as well. Understanding who you really are, what you think and feel, and why you feel the way you do only aids in your ability to understand where other people are coming from. And, knowing yourself inside out will help you see what is most important to you, what your priorities are, and any changes that you need to make in order to see your dreams realized. You are capable of anything, and you can make your life exactly what you want it to be.

Thank you again for wanting to master the power you have within yourself, and for taking the time to read the information provided to help you gain a new understanding of how to go about getting everything you aspire and aim for out of life.

Finally, if you found this book useful in anyway, a review on Amazon is always greatly appreciated!

Book #4

Manipulation

The Definitive Guide to Understanding

Manipulation, MindControl and NLP

Introduction

I want to thank you and congratulate you for purchasing the book, *"Manipulation: The Defining Guide to Understanding Manipulation, Mind Control, and NLP"*.

There are always instances, throughout life, where you can't get exactly what you desire, but you never need to settle for being disappointed. Instead, you can learn about manipulation and mind control, how to use it on others with NLP techniques, and spot when others are using it on you. Most people believe that manipulation is a negative thing, and the concept generally gets a bad rap, but that all depends on what type of manipulation you're using. In this book, we will go over the following:

- **Defining Manipulation:** As mentioned above, there is a lot of misunderstanding surrounding this word, what it means, how it's used, and more. In this guide, you will learn what you need to know about the concept of manipulation and general persuasion and influence.

- **The Benefits of Using it Right, and How to do that:** Manipulation can be used in a positive way that benefits all parties involved, but this is something you have to learn about to master.

- **How to Spot and Avoid Negative Manipulation:** If you aren't aware of what it looks like to be manipulated by others, it's almost certain that it will happen to you, which could be dangerous. Leaving yourself upon to the whim of whoever wishes to manipulate you could have long lasting harmful effects

Thanks again for purchasing this book, I hope you enjoy it!

Chapter 1:

What is Manipulation and How does it Work?

anipulation exists in everyone's life on the planet. Within the human mind, a few different groups of shortcuts exist that leave us vulnerable to manipulation, and there are countless combinations and variations of these. Many people are even willing to put their lives on the line for them, which is no exaggeration. Some people will pick a job they hate, drink poison, or risk their lives in war. They might even get into an accident on the street completely unaware that they are following through actions of a story they read in the paper the day before. Most importantly, they would be spending money and time.

What is Manipulation?

Manipulation is the influence a person uses to try to alter the perceptions or behaviors of others. Often, it's done through underhanded, deceptive, or abusive techniques, but not always. In some people's opinions, when a manipulator advances their own interests using these techniques, without consideration for the needs of others, the methods are exploitative.

- **Negative Manipulation:** This is when you intentionally withhold information from someone to get what you want, play up your own emotions in a false way to persuade someone, or otherwise threaten them indirectly for selfish reasons. Negative manipulation has harmed countless people in the world. Being under the negative manipulation of another person can make you feel like you're crazy, or act in ways that you would normally never act. We will cover this in more detail in later chapters.

- This method of manipulation relies on hidden agendas, ulterior motives, and attempts to force others to give into your will. Although the manipulator looks in control and strong on the surface, they often feel very insecure on the inside; otherwise they wouldn't need to engage in such behaviors. The actions of these people (such as disregarding and exploiting the rights of other people) are a signal of a lack of health, on a mental level. In fact, people who engage in these behaviors have a hard time finding and keeping positive relationships with others.

- **Positive (or Ethical) Manipulation:** Also known as persuasion or influence, this is when you convince someone to come around to your ways of thinking or acting, but in a way that also benefits them. This has a positive, rather than harmful, effect. There are a few clear distinctions between negative and positive manipulation, and it's important to make sure you know the difference. Everyone uses positive manipulation and influence to further our own goals with other people, which is perfectly fine and normal. This method of manipulation acknowledges the boundaries and rights of others, and uses honest and direct communication.

- This method of manipulation is a simple way to function efficiently and effectively in your environment, and to benefit and make use of the social order that exists in our world. It recognizes that other people have a basic integrity, and a choice of whether or not to follow through with your persuasion attempts. In essence, this acknowledges that each person should be autonomous and acknowledges a baseline of human respect between you and others. We are all social creatures who need each other, in one way or another.

What is NLP and How does it Relate to this?

NLP (or Neuro-Linguistic Programming) is a study that focuses on the elements that allow us to experience the world. These elements are programming, language, and the neurology of our brains. Our neurological systems control the way our physical bodies work, language regulates the way we communicate with the world and other people, and the programming we go through in life decides what our models of reality will look like. All of this determines who we will be, what we will think like, what our habits will be, and what type of lives we will lead. We will discuss, in more detail, NLP techniques in a later chapter of this book.

Being aware of these definitions allows you to use knowledge to better your life. When you are aware of what methods can be used to influence you, suddenly you are empowered to make choices about what does. This book will teach you how to recognize manipulation methods being used today, along with methods for resisting them. You will also learn about using the ingrained mental shortcuts we all have to persuade, manipulate, and influence others. Let's look at something we are all familiar with, advertising, to illustrate how this works.

Manipulation in Advertising vs. Personal Manipulation:

How exactly is manipulation in advertising done? Advertisers utilize many different techniques for manipulating customers or potential consumers. These include appeals to emotions and feelings, ads that are disguised as other forms of entertainment, and ads that appeal to insecurities or fears. As these strategies become more and more sophisticated and complex, consumers can recognize and resist the manipulative or deceptive tactics by learning more about how they work. In addition to this, you can apply this knowledge the techniques that people use to manipulate each other. Let's look at some of the manipulation techniques of advertising, to get a better understanding of this subject:

- **Emotional Reactions:** Advertisers know that emotions are a great way to elicit specific feelings in people, and they use this to their advantage. Advertisers often play up or emphasize the feelings that products will bring you, rather than actual characteristics or qualities of the products. In fact, a lot of ads aim to elicit a feeling response that distracts customers from considering the functionality or value of the product. They might show specific scenarios that consumers can remember or relate to in some other way, like your first child's birth, or a date. This increases the feeling response and engagement, emotionally, that viewers will feel with that product.

- This same technique is used in interpersonal manipulation. For example, a friend or significant other who is trying to convince you to do something you don't want to do might try to encourage you by telling you it will be fun, or even bringing up past memories to elicit a feeling response in you. Some may also use fear tactics to elicit a negative emotion, or a fear of a negative emotion in others to get them to do what they want. This is, for example, used often by parents who threaten their children with being punished unless they follow through on orders.

- **Ads Disguised as Simple Entertainment:** It becomes more and more common that ads disguise themselves as simple entertainment, providing depictions of humorous or relatable narratives to attract consumers. Skillful or clever screen writing, cute animal mascots, and unique or memorable strategies all help to make customers feel more engaged, and thus likelier to remember the product being advertised. Some ads will even show the most outrageous scenarios they can invent to make this happen. Companies that sell products that are unhealthy, like candy or beer, tend to utilize humor techniques to distract viewers from detrimental or negative factors of products.

- This type of technique used in advertising can be compared to interpersonal manipulation tactics which misrepresent true intentions. For example. Someone who is manipulating you might tell you that their intentions are something completely different than they really are. They might pretend to only wish to entertain or please you, when they truly have ulterior motives. They might also use flattery or other false narratives to further their own personal agenda.

- **Using Fear and Insecurity:** Advertisers are famous for preying on the insecurities of consumers. For example, TV commercials may depict a character that they wish to portray as "unattractive" or lesser than others by focusing on a particular "flaw", such as baldness, or yellowing teeth. They then appear to offer the magical solution to the problem by attempting to sell you their product. Another example of using fear as an ad tactic is advertising for soap or other cleaning products during times when sickness is prevalent. Many times, their products don't actually help combat the sickness at all.

- An example of this tactic being used in interpersonal relations is in romantic relationships. Perhaps one person is ready to break up and move on, but the other is afraid to live without them. Instead of respecting the person's choice to leave and move on with their life, they try to appeal to that person's insecurities by insinuating that they will never find someone as good. Fear is a perfect example of a negative manipulation tactic that is good to guard yourself against. We will show you how to do that later on in the book.

The Rule of Reciprocation, a Common Technique:

One common and famous technique for manipulating others using automatic or subconscious behavior, is called the rule of reciprocation. The basic idea behind this "rule" is that if someone else does something nice for you, you should do something for them in return. This is something we are all taught from childhood, either directly or indirectly, and is so ingrained that nearly nobody questions it. This tactic is used often to manipulate others.

- **Sample Counters:** Think about samples given out at grocery stores. The idea behind them is that if someone gives you a taste of something at no cost, your mind will see it as a favor and make you more likely to purchase their product. Instead of having people paid to walk around and ask people if they would like to buy something, they have people giving out free stuff, which makes others more obligated to listen to what the sales person has to say.

- **Door to Door Fundraisers:** Another area this tactic is used in is fundraising efforts. When someone goes door to door to try to collect donations from people, they are a lot more likely to get someone to listen to what they have to say (and therefore, at times, donate) if they offer something first. Simple techniques like this can make donations multiply and sky rocket, due to basic psychology manipulation techniques.

This rule applies to favors big and small and you don't necessarily feel obligated to return the same amount of "good" or favor back to someone who has done something for you. In fact, you can do someone a tiny favor, and then ask them for something big, and the trick still has an effect. For example, you could offer to help someone carry groceries in from their car, or mention that you have dedicated hours of your life to them (implying that they now owe you big.) Of course, this type of manipulation can be used for good aims, such as getting your child to do their schoolwork or study for a test, convincing your sick mother to go to the doctor, or getting your manager to give you a raise. These techniques can be used to discover the true reason behind issues going on at work or in the family, and help people move past harmful habits they are stuck in.

Ways of using these Techniques in Everyday Life:

There are important distinctions between NLP methods and the techniques listed above. A quality NLP method benefits people and incorporates mental tricks like the one mentioned above (reciprocity). However, you don't have to be aware of NLP or hypnosis methods to use manipulation techniques.

- **The Hypnotist Metaphor:** You might find it useful to think about the following metaphor. Envision being a hypnotist who must convince a patient or subject to stop moving and be completely still. You have to get them to look forward and ignore all noises besides your instructions. You could use techniques for building rapport, or trance techniques, which may or may not actually work.

- **Considering the Person:** It's important, when learning about or trying to partake in manipulation, to know your subject. If the person you are trying to get to focus, for example, has been employed by the military at one point, wearing official general clothes from their army and calling out "Attention!" will do the trick. Conditioning is something that is often with us for life, whether we are aware of it or not. This means that you are not creating new responses or reactions in the person, but simply calling upon something that already exists within them.

How are Mental Shortcuts related to Manipulation?

It's obvious why these behaviors are thought of as automatic reactions, but how are mental shortcuts related? In the language of NLP, this could be called distortion, deletion, or generalization, but we are going to keep it simple for now. Let's start with how human beings think and relate to the world, something everyone has firsthand experience with.

- **Shortcuts for Survival:** Our world is complicated and we are constantly surrounded by new stimuli. It's impossible for humans to constantly think about every factor that is needed, which is why certain processes are automated. Perhaps we would still survive without this, but it would be extremely inefficient. Think, for example, about operating your car. Can you recall when you first started driving, and the way you needed to pay close attention to every single part of the process? But now, it's simply automatic. This is done by utilizing mental shortcuts.

- Rather than having to stop and agonizingly consider every angle of every sign or light, you already know what to do instinctively due to repetition. Think now about reading information or news on the internet. How do you figure out whether stories you're reading are true or false? You aren't going to thoroughly research every article every time. Instead, you apply mental shortcuts to find your answer and opinion.

- **How these Shortcuts leave us Vulnerable:** This part is important. Not everyone realizes that they are employing these mental shortcuts throughout the day. They simply happen automatically, without much thought, after all that's the point of them, right? But this automated process of thinking and acting can leave us vulnerable to others who wish to manipulate these tendencies. Although we need these automatic processes and shortcuts for survival, to make decisions quickly with minimal thought and effort, they are often used against us.

- The examples above given of advertising manipulation tactics are a depiction of this at work, as are the tactics used by politicians during speeches. Everyone knows the terms "clearance" and "sale." When signs exclaiming either one of these are placed out front of a store, people know to expect good deals and bargains on their shopping trips. When we see an advert claiming that there is a limited time, great offer happening at their location, our subconscious minds pick up on this.

These mental shortcuts are all around us and a very important part of our lives. Statistics prove that a guy who is better looking will receive a less harsh conviction or sentence in court. Studies have shown that American citizens are far more likely to vote for someone who looks friendly and paternal, because of our mental associations of seeing people like this as more trustworthy. Salespeople will be more successful in their sales if they simply present their items in a certain way. We cannot control our own automatic thought processes and conditioning, but becoming aware of this is beneficial for many reasons.

Chapter 2:

The Benefits of Learning about this Skill

Learning about manipulation, both in its positive and negative forms, is important for any human who wishes to function in a healthy way. Using persuasion techniques from NLP studies can increase your ability to ethically manipulate others and be more influential, in general. Ethical manipulation is an important skill in life, and can be used for influencing clients, members of your family, or colleagues at work. Anyone who learns about NLP for this reason will access useful and powerful abilities to help support the process of ethical manipulation and persuasion.

The Benefits of Knowing about Persuasion and Manipulation:

Mastering these skills and the fine art of ethical manipulation will give you new opportunities for increases in your sales numbers, getting to know important or influential figures, better self-esteem, and the ability to express yourself naturally and authentically. The art of persuasion is an important part of the theory of communication, and these methods help create and foster healthy relations on a community level, along with customer and employee relations. When you are good at employing the correct use of argumentation, it will lead to raises, promotions, and influential or powerful positions. Let's look at a few more benefits to this:

- **Rapport:** One important benefit to learning about ethical manipulation is using it to build rapport with others. Rapport is what helps us feel at ease with another person, feel common ground, and look for qualities shared in common. It is necessary for all positive interactions and achieving goals that include other people. Essentially, this happens when you feel comfortable with someone, relate to them easily, and have a warm interaction with them. Rapport relies on seeing common ground between you and another person.

- It's an important aspect of persuasion and manipulation because people are a lot more likely to do favors for others, or simply agree with them, if they see that person as similar to themselves. Therefore, everyone who knows how to ethically persuade others is aware of building rapport. In this book, we will give you a few methods for doing this with many different types of people. No matter how different the person seems from you, it's possible to find common ground and build rapport if you simply know how.

- **Seeing the Needs and Wants of Others:** When you are effective at persuading other people, or knowing how to read signs of them trying to persuade, you catch a glimpse into what they find the most important. In this way, you can understand humanity on a deeper level, and use this information to get ahead in life. When you recognize others' wants and needs, not only do you better understand them as an individual, but you can become closer. This is what separates positive and negative manipulation.

- **Effective Communication:** Rapport-building and recognizing the needs of others are foundations that can lead to effective communication. Effectively communicating is useful for countless reasons, among which are conflict resolution, getting ahead in your career, and resolving conflicts on a professional and personal level. Let's look at the example of building healthy relations with employees from your work. Talking to them about benefit decreases, or impending layoffs, along with other unpleasant company decisions, requires a certain level of savvy that can be gained using ethical manipulation techniques.

- One method for dong this relies on reaching your listeners using logic and facts. You could, for example, show that if your business doesn't close down a certain property, the rest of your businesses will have to close down. The second method relies on the fact that your listeners are paying attention mostly on an emotional plane, rather than using logic. In situations like this, appealing to empathy by illustrating examples of families who will suffer as a result of not taking action is more effective. As mentioned earlier in the book, knowing your audience is important for effectively persuading people.

- **Finding Shared Values with Anyone:** There are times, in life, when we are forced to work along with or spend time with people who seem very different from us. When you are effective at persuasion and ethical manipulation, this becomes easy. You can simply find shared values with them, no matter how different they appear to be on the surface. This allows you access to the skills of lightening tension in tough situations, or getting people to do you favors readily. People are more likely to help those who they see as similar to them, meaning that knowing how to find similarities is a must for interpersonal relations.

- **Beating Resistance:** Marketing depends entirely on the buying habits of consumers. One hard habit to beat is buyer resistance in consumers. Effectively persuading buyers means helping them to feel at ease with their choices, while simultaneously improving your sales numbers. A main factor in doing this is displaying to the buyer your understanding of the hard choice they are facing. Letting them know that you are aware of how difficult the purchase is and understand their feelings can allow them to let down their guard.

- This allows the buyer to see you more as a human. They may then make a purchase that benefits them and you, as the sales person. This of course applies not just to sales, but to interpersonal situations. Empathizing with another person is a great way to get them to open up, feel more comfortable, and become decisive about important choices.

- **Expressing Yourself more Effectively:** Skills in influence and positive manipulation helps individuals to express themselves authentically. Constructing logical and sound arguments that people come to agree with creates and sustains self-assuredness and confidence. Arguments that use logic rely on facts, not just opinions. Even though a person might start with a certain idea or opinion, researching the situation or material will allow them a chance to give others important and valid data and information. Speakers who are truly powerful and influential use facts to support their arguments, and use that information to prove that they are correct.

Techniques for Persuasion and Manipulation Skills:

This book will go over many different techniques for this, but let's start with the following basics:

- **Mirroring:** This is one of the quickest ways to build rapport with someone you just met. You pay attention to their bodily movements, tone of voice, and values, and mirror them subtly. For example, if someone is standing with their arms crossed, do the same thing. If they are speaking excitedly and quickly, match their tone and pitch. This must be done in a very subtle way or it will have the opposite effect you're hoping for. The reason why this is so effective is because you can eventually have someone follow you to a conclusion or decision that you wish for them to reach.

- **Questioning:** Another technique for this is discovering what people need and want by asking questions. You do this to elicit their personal values and figure out what they think is most important in this world, then you can appeal to those values by aligning your idea, service, or product with what they find important.

- **Honesty:** This is a key difference in ethical manipulation and negative, selfish manipulation. Effective influence and persuasion rely on honesty and transparency. Real, genuine, positive persuasion makes no attempt to fool the audience, but rather gives a grouping of facts and information that the audience can consider to make the best choice. Learning the skill of effective influence using solid communication techniques can drastically improve self-esteem levels, job performance, and chances of securing positions of leadership.

Influence and persuasion should always be used for helping others, rather than hurting them. False information shouldn't be used or given, and if you have a good understanding of true ethical manipulation, it will never be necessary. There are many benefits to gain from learning about NLP, including an extreme increase in your persuasion abilities, which might be the most important social skill you could develop. Since NLP techniques are so valuable, that is what we'll be focusing on in much of this guide. This chapter was intended to illustrate how important this skill is, so hopefully you now have a fuller understanding of the subject.

Chapter 3:

Manipulation and Influence Techniques

The simplest and easiest method for manipulating others, particularly American citizens, is by appealing to their feelings. Although you can use logic to help people reach a logical decision, you can also guide them in feeling particular emotions that lead to the results you want. This is the essence of manipulation. This book will cover a wide variety of techniques to use for this, but first we are going to cover some tips that get you into the right frame of mind for persuading others. Here are some techniques and tips to help you along:

- **Get a Hold of your Own Feelings First:** It can be easier to influence or ethically manipulate someone who is more on the indecisive side, but you can also persuade people with a strong resolve to consider and come over to your point of view. Being aware of your own feelings and how they come across to others is an important part of this. In order to persuade others, you have to be relatable to them, and in order to be relatable, you have to know which emotions to show, how, and when.

- For example, accessing a confident state of mind when interacting with someone makes you come across as calm and collected, meaning that others, especially indecisive people, will gladly follow your lead. Exhibiting your adventurous or authoritative qualities can be especially influential when you're around someone who is more on the shy side. The key lies in knowing which personality traits to show and when and who to do that around.

- **Become Charismatic:** Throwing tantrums and crying to get your way might work for some, but being charismatic and having people like you is a much better way to exert influence and effectively manipulate the feelings others have of you. It's also a good way to reach for mutually beneficial outcomes to your persuasion. Charm is a foundational part of this. When you are likeable in the majority of situations, reacting with strong emotions in specific situations will have more impact on others. So study up on becoming more charismatic, dress well, and make sure you treat others with respect. All of that will help you be more influential.

- Being charismatic is all about getting people to feel comfortable around you. You can do this by showing that you care about them. Instead of simply talking about what you like and what you think, ask people for their input and opinions. This shows that you value them as a person and think they are worth listening to. In addition to this, make sure you make eye contact during conversations, but not too much. Essentially, you should be looking directly at someone's face for at least 60 percent of the conversation.

- **Humanize Yourself to Others:** One way to get others to trust you and open up to you more easily is to humanize yourself to them. One way to do this is to share personal information with them that is relevant and allows them to feel as though you trust them with something. When this happens, they are more likely to open up to you and allow you to influence them. This is similar to, and draws off of, the technique of reciprocation discussed in an earlier chapter of the book.

- People automatically like you more when you decide to confide something in them. Depending on the situation, this will vary, so use your judgment. For example if you are trying to persuade someone to trust your advice as a veterinarian, you could share a personal anecdote about having to put your lifelong companion, Fluffy, down when you were a kid, and how it all worked out for the best. If you wish for your friend to take your advice on a breakup, relate a story about a hard time you went through that is similar in nature.

- **Positivity:** When you are attempting to persuade or ethically manipulate another person, your worst enemy is doubt. You should maintain positive relations with the person you're talking to, and never resort to attacking or negativity. Not only does this poison possible relations between you and the other person, but it makes you a very ineffective influencer. Show your best qualities to make yourself relatable and likeable.

- **Mention Advantages and Benefits:** Getting people to come around to a specific way of thinking or acting often means you must display good reasons for them to do so. Mention explicit benefits and advantages to them coming around to your opinion on the matter. If you're trying to sell something to someone, for example, list the worries that they will be free from with your product.

There are many different ways to manipulate, control, and influence the feeling response that people have to you. Realizing this is the essence of leadership and true influence. Perhaps the most important skill of all is being a likeable person. Now that we have covered some of the benefits to manipulation (when used in a positive and uplifting manner), it's time to discuss some of the negative and harmful effects that irresponsible manipulation can lead to.

Chapter 4:

How to Recognize Negative Manipulation

One of the most important parts of learning about manipulation is figuring out how to protect yourself from it. Nearly everyone in this world has been manipulated negatively in some way or another, and it never feels good or nice. Everyone on this planet just wants to meet their own needs, but people who use negative manipulation use deceit and underhanded techniques for doing so, instead of honesty and an approach of mutual benefit. In essence, they don't care about your wants or needs, and only wish to serve themselves. This relies on subtly influencing another person with abusive, deceptive, or hidden tactics.

Veiled Hostility and Intimidation Tactics:

At first, it might come across as flattering, friendly, and harmless, like that person only has your best interests at heart, but that is never the case with negative manipulation. Sometimes, it's barely concealed hostility, and when someone uses these abusive techniques, they are trying to gain power over you. At times, you might not even know that you're being intimidated subconsciously. When you're used to manipulation from childhood or the past, it can be more difficult to recognize it or know what's happening because it's familiar and might even feel natural in some ways. You may feel an instinctual anger or discomfort, while the manipulator uses reasonable, ingratiating, or pleasant terms that appeal to your sympathy or guilt. This leads to you overriding your gut feelings and not knowing how to respond.

Who uses these Negative Tactics?

People in codependent relationships might have a hard time being assertive or direct, leading to the use of negative manipulation to achieve their personal goals. These types might also become victims of narcissists or sociopaths. Abusive partners might use these tactics, as well.

How to Recognize Negative Manipulation:

There are a few tactics that every manipulator uses, and these are favors and gifts, flattery, over the top apologies, fake sympathy, false concern, evasion techniques or avoidance, blackmail, making assumptions about you, playing with your mind, undermining your thoughts and feelings, bribing you, blaming you, faking innocence, making excuses, comparing, complaining, and guilt tripping. Let's look at a few of these techniques in detail:

- **Favors with "Strings Attached":** They will often utilize the technique of guilt either directly or in an implied way. They do you favors and then hold them over your head later when they want something from you.

- **Getting Power through Sympathy:** Some negative manipulators will deny agreements, conversations, or promises they made you. They might also intentionally start fights and then blame you in order to gain power by upsetting you.

- **Bribery:** Bribery is very commonly used by parents in order to get their kids to follow their instructions. For example, your parents might bribe you to go to the school they want you to attend, by buying you a new car.

- **Using Assumptions:** Negative manipulators will often make assumption aloud about you or your beliefs or intentions, and then respond to those assumptions. They will ignore what you say to the contrary as a way to justify their actions and feelings. They might even pretend as though you have agreed or decided something to effectively ignore your objections or input on the subject. For example, they will tell you how you feel, and respond to that, instead of asking you how you feel and listening.

- **Pressured Reciprocation:** We discussed the influence tactic of reciprocation, where you offer someone something small and then follow up with a larger request. This can be harmless, but when it's used with pressure or guilt, that's when it becomes a negative manipulation tactic. When you say no to their request, they will turn around and try to make themselves out to be the victim. It will be all about the manipulator and their personal issues, leading you to feel defensive.

- They will then bring up past occurrences of you not fulfilling their wishes, and lay a lot of blame on you to try to get you to agree with what they want. They don't care if it hurts you at all, in fact, as long as it makes you do what they want. You get the feeling, when it comes to a negative manipulator, that there are always hidden motives or strings attached when they offer something to you or act kind.

- **False Concern or Blackmail:** This is a tactic, which relies on "well-meaning worry", that is intended to make you doubt yourself or to invalidate your choices. The negative manipulator might also use shame, threats, intimidation, or anger tactics to get you to do what they want. They may shame you to make you feel doubt and insecurity, even masking this with a false compliment. People who use blackmail might also use anger to scare you, leading you to putting aside your wants and needs to do what they want.

- If this method doesn't work on you, they might switch suddenly to a more positive mood and act nice toward you. This could lead you to feel relieved and become willing to do what they ask you to do. They may also bring up shameful memories from your past and threaten to tell others about it if you don't comply with their wishes. This may lead the victim of the negative manipulation to feel fearful to say no. If they say no, they will likely experience insults from the manipulator, such as being called selfish.

- **Passive Aggressive Manipulation**: Some people, especially those who are on the shy side, use passive manipulation tactics, since most people with codependent personalities are not very assertive. They might act agreeable on the surface, telling people what they want to hear, and then break their agreements later on. Instead of responding honestly to an issue that could lead to fighting or some type of confrontation, they avoid instead, try to change the subject, or deny and blame, using rationalizations and excuses.

- They are afraid to be wrong, and due to finding it difficult to raise conflict, they say yes even when they don't agree, and then follow up with complaints or guilt trips about how hard it will be to accommodate the other person. When someone confronts them, they may feel shame and have a hard time claiming responsibility for their actions. So instead, they create excuses, blame others, or try to "fix" things by apologizing, even if they don't mean it.

- Even these passive tactics, which aren't as obvious as the tactics of anger or shaming, are a method for expressing hostile feelings. These could involve saying yes to a request and then "forgetting" to follow through on it, because you never wanted to in the first place.

- **Self-Pity and Criticism**: Negative manipulators might use flattery and charm, offering to do nice favors for you, help with something you need assistance with, or give you gifts in order to gain your love and acceptance. Then they will turn around and use manipulation tactics like self-pity, guilt, and criticism to get others to follow along with their desires. "Why are you always so selfish? I help you when you need it." They constantly pull the victim card.

The best way to figure out a defense against manipulation is to know who you're dealing with and going up against. Every negative manipulator has different tactics, and if they know you well, they're already aware of what triggers you. Become aware of their methods for doing this and learn to recognize it when they attempt to use them on you. Build up your self-respect and self-worth, which will be your greatest defense.

Chapter 5:

How to Avoid being Manipulated

Now that we have gone over some of the methods and tactics people use to negatively manipulate others, it's time to talk about how to avoid these methods. Negative manipulation can be defined as convincing others to do whatever you desire, without offering something of value back to them. How does this phenomenon work?

• **A Threat and no Value:** If a person says, "Help me finish this project or I'm going to be angry with you," they are trying to negatively manipulate your actions. They are not actually offering anything of value to you in return. However, if a friend offers you something of value in return for a favor, that isn't negative manipulation, because you're getting something back for the effort you put in.

• **Making another Responsible for their Emotions:** Another form of manipulation is telling someone that they are responsible for how you feel and that they should feel guilty for that. For example, telling them that if they don't come to your party, you will be highly disappointed. This implies that it's their fault how you feel. However, if you offer to introduce your friend to someone they have been wanting to meet at your party, you are offering a situation that allows both of you to win.

Why do People Manipulate?

What are people's reasons for manipulating others? These can be anything from innocent and even friendly reasons to mean and selfish, but for the sake of this chapter, we're going to focus on negative and selfish manipulation.

• **Misery Likes Company:** They do it because they gain satisfaction, on an emotional level, from seeing the frustrated or otherwise negative responses of others. Certain people are so unhappy with their lives and themselves that they try to bring others down by creating problems for them.

- **It makes them feel Powerful:** Someone who is insecure and feels powerless will often try to exert power in other areas to make up for it. Getting others to do what they want gives them temporary satisfaction.

- **A Lack of Importance:** Another reason why people negatively manipulate others is because they don't think that they are important. They believe that if they simply request what they wish for, they won't get it because they don't matter enough. So instead, they try to make us feel ashamed or guilty as a consequence for not doing what they want, as a preemptive measure from disappointment.

- **They are "too Good" for some Things:** Other negative manipulators simply think that they are too good for certain tasks. They might see other people as below them, and therefore expect those people to do the tasks that they don't want to do. This could be due to laziness, or simply an inflated sense of self.

- **Not Knowing how to get Things done:** Some negative manipulators don't think that they are capable of gaining what they want, and instead operate under the assumption that they must convince and pressure others to do their bidding for them.

- **Selfishly "Helping" Others:** Other negative manipulators actually convince themselves that what they are doing will help people. This is a common idea embraced by people who think that they know better than others what is best for everyone. Due to their beliefs that they have a higher intelligence or ability, they feel satisfied doing this, and convince themselves that the people being manipulated are better off for it.

Actually, the majority of negative manipulators are not actually bad people; they are simply misguided, inconsiderate, insensitive, selfish, and often times, weak and insecure. Some of them believe that the people they are manipulating are not as valuable as themselves, and that their desires and needs are not as important. This mistaken belief is what allows them to continue to act the way they do without considering the feelings of other people.

Different types of Negative Manipulation:

- **Turning your Emotions against you:** Techniques for manipulation vary widely, but usually, negative manipulators will attempt to get the feelings of others to work against them. They will try to do that by doing or saying things that are intended to stir up fear, anger, shame, guilt, or any other uncomfortable feeling. For example, they might insinuate that if we don't follow through on their suggestions or orders, something horrible will result.

- **Threats of Future Unpleasantness:** They might also try to describe to you all of the different types of unpleasant situations that could arise if you don't do what they want. They might imply or even overtly insist that something is our fault, responsibility, or duty, using ethics and morality to pressure us to come around to their ideas or demands. Some people will even throw every trick at us, warning us of the consequences of disappointing or letting them down.

- **Common Phrases Used:** They may imply to us that we will be so happy if we do what they want us to do, or that we will make them very happy, and that they will love us so much. They may also use phrases like "You need to…" or "You must…" or "You should…" as a way to subtly pressure you into following through on what they are asking of you. They will say those phrases and others which insinuate great consequences if you don't follow the obligation they are giving to you.

What do each of the above methods and techniques share in common with each other? The person doing the negative manipulation doesn't offer anything of value in return for fulfilling their wishes. Instead, the victim gets exploited by a created power imbalance.

How to Avoid being Negatively Manipulated by Others:

So, now that we have discussed some of the signs of negative manipulation, it's time to figure out how to avoid it and recognize when someone is trying to use it on you.

- **Be Aware of your Rights:** The absolute most important rule you can follow when dealing with someone who wants to manipulate you in negative ways is to know your own worth and rights. This way, you will always know when someone is attempting to violate them. So long as others are not getting harmed in the process, you should be defending yourself. Every human should have the right to have differing opinions from others, to protect yourself, to say "no" when you need to, and to decide what's important to you. You should also have the right of expressing your wants, opinions, and feelings, and always be treated with respect.

- Unfortunately, the world has plenty of people who won't want to acknowledge or respect your rights, especially negative manipulators. You will also come into contact with others who generally wish to take advantage at any opportunity. However, you can proudly defy this by letting them know that you are the one who runs your life, no one else.

- **Maintain Healthy Distance:** Another way to tell who is manipulative is to pay attention to the way someone acts in varying situations and in front of various individuals. Although everyone, to a degree, puts on different faces depending on where they are, most people who are harmfully manipulative are extreme about it. They might, for example, be extremely polite and friendly to one person, and completely disrespect another, or act like a victim one second, and then act controlling immediately after.

- If you notice someone acting this way regularly, it's a good sign to distance yourself from them and not engage with them unless it's an absolute necessity. Usually, the reasons behind these types of behavior are complicated, and it isn't your duty or responsibility to help or change that person. Trying to do so will often only lead to suffering on your part, so it's better not to expect much when you notice these signs.

- **Don't Blame yourself:** A person who wishes to manipulate others in harmful ways searches for weaknesses to exploit, so it makes sense that someone who has been victimized by one might blame themselves or feel inadequate. But in a situation like this, you should remember that it isn't you that's the issue here; you are being pressured to feel bad by someone else who is very good at making people feel bad.

- This is how they get their way. Instead, think about the relationship you have with this person and ask yourself if they are respecting you, demanding reasonable things of you, and whether you are both benefiting, or only one of you is. Ask yourself, also, if you feel good about yourself after spending time with this person, or if you would feel better being around them less. The way you answer these questions will lead to important answers about where the issue lies in the situation.

- **Questioning them:** Eventually, this type of person is going to demand or request things from you. Many times, these requests or others will take their needs into consideration, while completely ignoring yours. Next time you receive a solicitation that is completely unreasonable, turn the focus back to them by asking some questions. Ask them if their request is reasonable, or if what they are asking from you is fair. You can also try asking if you get to have an opinion in this matter, or ask what benefit you will be gaining from the arrangement.

- Each time you ask questions like this, you are holding a mirror up to them, allowing them to see what they are truly asking of you. If they are self-aware, they will likely retract their request or demand. But there may be some cases, such as dealing with a narcissist, who will keep insisting without even considering your questions. If that happens, follow these guidelines.

- **Don't Answer Immediately:** One way to combat manipulation is to use time as a resource. Often, the manipulator will not only ask you to fulfill an unreasonable demand, but they will want an answer immediately. When this happens, rather than answering right away, use time and distance yourself from their request and influence. This can be done by telling them that you will think about it. Although these words are simple, they give your power back to you, giving you the option to weigh the advantages and disadvantages of the situation and let you work out something better, if need be.

- **Teach yourself to say "No" when needed:** Saying "no" is difficult for many people, since we are often taught and conditioned to be polite whenever possible. Being able to confidently but politely say "no" comes with learning communication skills. When this is articulated effectively, you can hold onto your self-respect, and also continue a healthy relationship. Keep in mind that your personal rights include deciding what matters to you, being able to turn down a request free from guilt, and choosing health and happiness for yourself. You are responsible for your life, not the person who is making unreasonable demands of you.

- **Create a Consequence:** Next time a negative manipulator tries to violate your rights, and refuses to accept your answer, set a consequence for their behavior. Knowing how to assert and identify appropriate consequences is a crucial skill for standing down someone who is being very difficult or disrespectful. If you can articulate this clearly and thoroughly, your consequences will cause them to pause and stop violating you, shifting to a position of respect.

How to Confront a Bully in a Safe Way:

Not all manipulators resort to bullying, but many of them do. Someone is being a bully when they use intimidation or harm to get what they want from you. Remember, always, that a bully chooses people they see as weak to pick on, and compliance and passivity will only strengthen this. However, a lot of bullies are afraid and insecure deep down, so when their victim starts to stand up for themselves, this will often lead the bully to back off. Whether this situation is occurring in a playground or at the office, it applies, most of the time. Keep in mind that many bullies have actually withstood bullying and violence. Although this doesn't excuse their behaviors, it does help the victim to understand.

Chapter 6:

A Guide to Positive Manipulation (Persuasion)

Leadership and manipulation go together, but there is a distinct difference between the type of manipulation discussed in the last chapter, and ethical (or positive) manipulation. Positive manipulation relies on using personal influence to gain a response or outcome. To put it another way, it relies on convincing someone to do what you are asking. This definition makes it easy to understand why the most powerful leaders in the world are often very skilled at ethical manipulation. Regardless of its negative connotations, manipulation is not always a bad thing. Actually, countless leaders in business could enjoy advantages from using some of these methods in their set of skills. One of these skills is using manipulation in a responsible, ethical, and positive way.

What makes Positive Manipulation Ethical?

Positive, ethical manipulation methods have outcomes and goals that have been thoroughly defined, and are always motivated by goal-seeking and accomplishment. It's not appropriate at all to try to manipulate people for pleasure or your own personal achievement, while disregarding their rights or desires. But it is necessary and appropriate to use this tactic as a way to help people achieve shared visions and to further an organization or business.

What to use Positive Manipulation Methods for:

Influence and persuasion skills are extremely useful and powerful for many different reasons. They can be used to convince a child to follow through on something, to change ideas in a county or community, or to help change the minds or actions of employees and customers at work. When you decide to develop these skills and methods, you instantly increase your own personal influence, leadership abilities, and power.

- **Influence:** Ethical manipulation mainly relies on persuading or influencing others to follow through on something they wouldn't do on their own. This could be thoughts or actions, and although the person might naturally choose something else, a leader who ethically manipulates them exerts subtle and appropriate pressure in order to help that person reach an outcome that is most desired.

- **Persuasion:** Subordinates and leaders often disagree on objectives, processes, and concepts, and this is entirely natural. But using techniques that rely on positive and ethical manipulation can help persuade peers or subordinates to come over to the way you think of things. Instead, of overtly pressuring, bullying, or bulldozing, these methods allow you to share your ideas and give them a chance to agree with you or shift to your perspective.

- **Inspiration:** When someone uses manipulation and has the correct motivation behind it, it can actually be very inspiring to the people involved. If, for example, you're looking at a difficult, long project, you can give the team some easy simple projects now in order to help them feel more capable and confident. This is, technically, manipulation, but it's for a good cause and helps the people involved. Manipulation is all about getting people to feel or act in certain ways. For example, getting people to be enthusiastic and exciting about something they are doing.

- **Unity:** Conflicts at work and home are a natural part of social interaction. But it's perfectly possible to manipulate a situation in order to bring about more unity. This relies on recognizing that a conflict is about to happen and finding ways to manipulate the situation to prevent problems. This is a great example of manipulation being a positive, rather than negative, influence. People who can do this are often seen as valuable assets to group situations or work environments, because they know how to mediate and keep the peace. These are valuable abilities to have.

- **For Defending yourself:** There are many benefits to learning about persuasion. Not only is it useful for using it yourself to get things done, but you can use it to protect yourself from manipulation that isn't good for you. For example, perhaps a friend is pressuring you to go out and drink all night when you have to be to work the next morning, just because they don't have to work. Being aware of persuasion tactics will help you to recognize theirs and persuade them to drop the subject. You can also use these tactics to exert your own will and rights in difficult situations.

- You can study your surroundings and the people around you in order to find the correct methods for getting done what you need to do. This can be at work, at home, or in your personal friendships and romantic relationships.

Why Compliance Manipulation is Ineffective:

In this section of the book, we're going to consider some main techniques for persuasion that can be used in nearly any situation. But before getting into these methods, we should go over what persuasion means to have a fuller understanding of it. This is crucial to be aware of, since persuasion can often be confused with pressuring others into compliance. The latter is often focused only on changing the behaviors of other people, while persuasion tactics try to get people or groups or people to feel and think positively about the thoughts or actions you wish for them to have.

- **Manipulation for Compliance:** There are lots of ways to manipulate people into complying with your ideas. Some examples of this include threats of legal action if you don't follow laws (like a ticket for not wearing your seatbelt), or a parent threatening their child with punishment for not finishing their homework or cleaning up their room. These are distinctly different from typical techniques for persuasion, because a change of feelings or beliefs is not necessary for the people to act or change their behaviors. They only have to be able to feel the fear and recognize it to comply.

- **Resentment and a Lack of Motivation:** The problem with techniques like the ones listed above is that without the fear or threat, people wouldn't follow through on what they're being asked to do. In addition to this, nobody enjoys being negatively manipulated, meaning that they are more likely to feel resentful of these tactics once they realize what is happening to them. Sadly, this form of manipulation is still very common, but although it can work for some cases, it's not a very sophisticated or effective tool.

When you look back at being manipulated into compliance, either by authority figures at school, bosses at work, or your own parents in childhood, it usually isn't a very good feeling. More often than not, it leads to negative feelings and interactions, and this is because it's based on fear, instead of free will and choice. The question then becomes, how is it possible to get people to do what you want them to do of their own volition? They must make the choice themselves if they are going to continue to choose it.

Using NLP and Creating Agreement for Successful Positive Manipulation:

The trick here is to use agreement to be successful at positive manipulation and persuasion. You have to create a few different levels of agreement, such as spiritual, emotional, mental, and physical. Consider an individual getting carried on by a strong current of water, such as a river. You have to construct a strong enough agreement stream that it pulls the person in your direction. How is this possible to do?

- **Connect:** Studies done in hypnosis and NLP show that establishing rapport with someone else makes them much more agreeable to your ideas, suggestions, and actions. This can be done by subtly mirroring them, as mentioned earlier in the book. Don't think of it as imitating or mocking, but rather as complementing the other person's facial expressions and gestures. This gives them more positive feelings towards you and makes them more suggestible to your ideas.

- If you practice this often and truly understanding the concepts behind establishing connection and rapport with others, you can utilize mirroring and matching as a technique to bring others into positive alignment with yourself. Furthermore, this can be done in such a way that the other individual has no idea that you're using a technique at all. That's because this is a subliminal method that everyone responds to in spite of themselves. This leads to a nice, warm, harmonious sense that the two of you are relating to each other.

- **Trust:** Not many people are aware of the way that nonverbal communication happens between two people, even though this is where the majority of signals are being sent. When you mirror and match someone else's mannerisms and expressions, their subconscious is receiving a message that it's okay to trust you and let their guard down. This is because you are acting like them, and most humans relate easier to people that they see as similar to them. Even if the person doesn't know why on a conscious level, they will feel more comfortable with you.

- Trust is necessary for getting someone to come around to your ideas or goals. It's true that you can pressure someone into going along with what you want, but if there is any chance that they will enjoy it and do it willingly, you have to create rapport and positive feelings in your interactions. Only then is persuasion or ethical manipulation possible.

- **Breaking Patterns:** In addition to mirroring to build rapport, other NLP techniques exist for strong subliminal influence. One example of this is using questions in order to re-direct someone's attention or focus to something else, or to break mental patterns. Questions are effective because they are hard to resist answering. Our minds automatically want to try to solve questions as soon as they are asked. For example, if someone asks you what good things have happened in your life lately, your state of mind automatically begins focusing on positivity.

- **Storytelling and Metaphors:** Another method for persuading others is using storytelling and metaphors to get your point or idea across to them. People who specialize in persuasion can make this tactic very complicated, but it's actually effective right away, in a lot of cases. This can be done by sharing a story that shows you reaching a conclusion that you are hoping they will also reach, using positive descriptive terms. Make sure you are making something sound highly positive, if you want someone to agree with you.

- **Set a Goal:** If you have any desires to accomplish something specific, you have to get specific about defining it. It's too easy to meander through interactions and daily life without having a clear cut vision of what you wish to do. In order to effectively persuade and ethically manipulate others, set a desired goal for the interaction you have with them. This could be to simply call or text them, send a letter in the mail, set up a meeting, or convince them to sign up for something. Decide ahead of time what the action or outcome will be that you wish for the individual to come around to.

- **Get Confident and Passionate:** Become enthusiastic about your service, product, idea, or concept. Enthusiasm is contagious and effective for persuasion. Think about it, when you're talking to someone who is trying to convince you about something, is it easier to listen to them when they are droning on and seem bored out of their minds, or when they seem completely sold on and excited about the idea? It's important to get excited. This can be done by emotionally connecting with whatever advantages and benefits you are providing with your idea. Think about who the idea has helped and will help.

- In addition to this, giving logical perspectives is also helpful when it comes to ethical manipulation and persuading people. Keep in mind that people often make their choices based on emotion, and later justify those choices using logical reasons. Appealing to both of these is your best bet.

- **Be Upfront and Ask Directly:** Another technique is to simply ask directly for whatever it is that you want. This might mean a date, asking someone to buy your product, or convincing them to sign up for something. If you don't ask, you will never know! A lot of times, people simply don't know what to do, and offering an action, idea, or solution can be helpful for everyone involved.

Practice all of the skills listed above to help your influence and persuasion skills develop and grow into strong abilities. Becoming great with persuasion and ethical manipulation relies first on understanding the foundations of persuasion, and then using techniques to support them. Keep in mind that as long as you are offering something of value in return for what you are asking of someone, you are using persuasion and influence in a positive way. Being aware of what persuasion and manipulation tactics look like can also help protect you against people trying to use them adversely against you.

Conclusion

Thank you again for purchasing this book!

I hope this book was able to help you to understand how prevalent and important the subject of manipulation is in our everyday lives. Although the word "manipulation" typically has a negative connotation, it isn't always that way. We encounter this phenomenon far more often than we consciously realize, and living the most advantageous life possible means getting in touch with this and using it to your benefit.

With the information in this book, you will never again be taken advantage of by manipulative people without your best interests at heart. In addition to this, you can utilize methods of positive and ethical manipulation to influence and lead others in beneficial ways. When you understand this tool of social power and influence, you can achieve whatever it is you wish to achieve in life. Our worlds are increasingly connected and social, so this is an invaluable skill to develop. Luckily, it can be learned and constantly improved, like any other skill in life.

Finally, if you enjoyed this book, then I'd like to ask you for a favor, would you be kind enough to leave a review for this book on Amazon? It'd be greatly appreciated!

Thank you!

Before you go, I just wanted to say thank you for purchasing my book.

You could have picked from dozens of other books on the same topic but you took a chance and chose this one.

So, a HUGE thanks to you for getting this book and for reading all the way to the end.

Now I wanted to ask you for a small favor. **Could you please take just a few minutes to leave a review for this book?**

This feedback will help me continue to write the type of books that will help you get the results you want. So if you enjoyed it, please let me know! (-:

www.ingramcontent.com/pod-product-compliance
Lightning Source LLC
Chambersburg PA
CBHW061757260326
41914CB00006B/1141